Flowering plants for

indoors + balconies

bloom

For our blooming wonderful families

We are proud to acknowledge the Gadigal people of the Eora Nation as the Traditional Custodians of the Country on which we have written this book. We recognise their continuing connection to the plants and ecosystems of this region, which they have cared for since time immemorial, and their role as this land's first storytellers. We pay our respects to Elders past and present. Sovereignty has never been ceded.

Flowering plants for indoors + balconies

bloom

Lauren Camilleri + Sophia Kaplan of *Leaf Supply*

Smith
Street
Books

contents

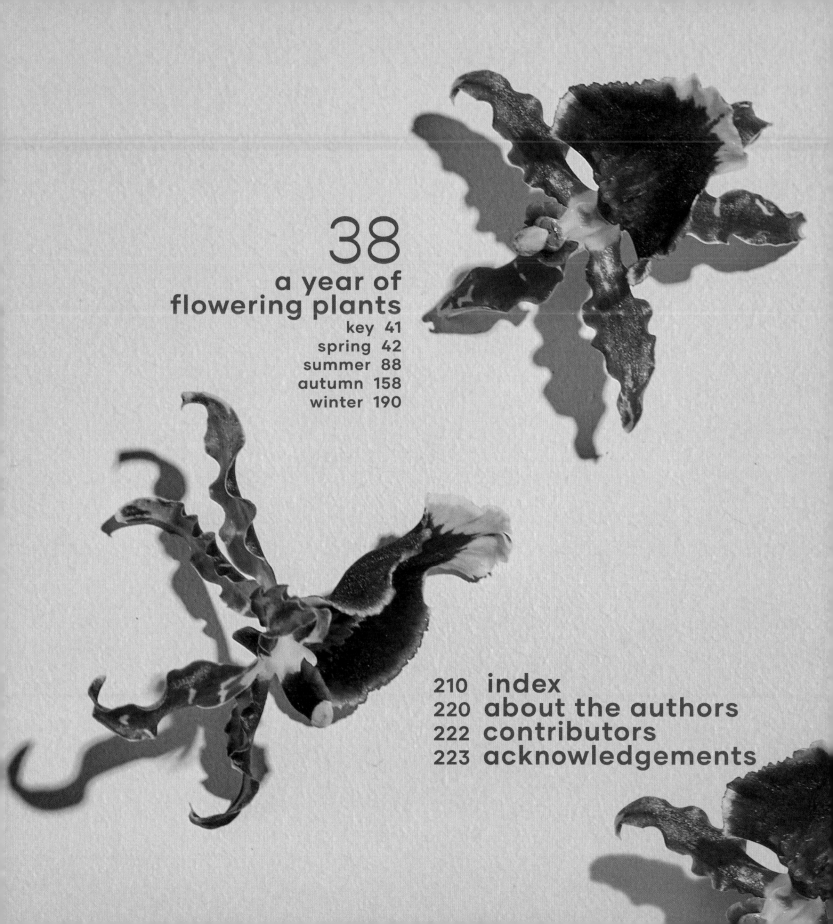

38 a year of flowering plants

the alluring nature of flowers

Flowers and the plants that produce them have captivated humans and pollinators alike for eons. The beauty and sheer variety of flowering plants is a testament to the mastery of nature; they are a celebration of form, colour, texture and scent.

A HELLEBORE THROWS DRAMATIC DANCING SHADOWS

From the tiniest of translucent orchids to the enormous bird-like pelican flower (*Aristolochia grandiflora*), nearly 400,000 species of flowering plants have been documented so far.

While many of these plants are grown for food, fibre or medicine, when we think of flowers it is generally more for their cultural significance. They form important parts of religious rituals, from temple offerings to funeral processions, and feature in many famous artworks, songs and books. And, of course, they have been given as gifts for centuries and are imbued with meaning – a 'language of flowers' so to speak.

While all this romance is an important part of the story, flowers also serve a very practical purpose as the reproductive organ of a plant. Evolution has spurred flowers to develop into attractive lures to would-be pollinators. Strong perfume, bright colours and bold shapes, along with more subtle compositions, all work to woo insects and birds to aid in pollination. In other instances, their design helps facilitate self-pollination. Regardless of the method, flowers are key to ensuring the survival of the species, and are a fundamental component of our ecosystem. Understanding the science of flowers, their anatomy and purpose, is not only fascinating, but helps to set the groundwork for any gardening endeavours.

While all this romance is an important part of the story, flowers also serve a very practical purpose.

Caring for plants and watching them thrive is a therapeutic undertaking that brings great pleasure to many. Inevitably they sometimes also wither, a part of the process that must also be respected. Although getting plants to flower indoors often takes some coaxing, understanding their care requirements will help build your confidence as a gardener and give you a greater chance of achieving this beautiful show. From light and water to soil and fertiliser, we've collected our best tips and tricks to help you along the way.

Flowers are fleeting bursts of joy. Like a living calendar, they help illustrate the passing of time. We'll guide you through the seasons to show you how to grow an indoor or balcony garden that will bloom and capture your heart throughout the year. In spring, bulbs such as tulips push forth from deep, wide pots planted out in autumn, and dainty little oxalis and geranium flowers begin to appear. By summer, hoyas and begonia are hitting their peak, and hydrangeas can be brought indoors for their showy flowering period before being returned to sunnier positions on balconies for the rest of the year. Autumn heralds sweet cyclamen, Japanese anemone and a wide range of orchids, while succulents such as little pickles and kalanchoe, largely blooming in winter, add colour to cold days.

Now more than ever it is important that we pay respect to our flora and appreciate its key role in keeping our planet alive.

We have been lucky enough to peek inside the gardens and minds of some amazing plant people. Flower queen Petrina Burrill has cultivated an enchanting, bloom-filled garden in inner-city Melbourne. The happiness Petrina exudes is surely influenced by the containers overflowing with field flowers she enjoys in situ or arranged into beautiful bouquets. Jane Rose Lloyd, who is also the insightful and invaluable horticultural consultant on this book, has a serious passion for plants and an admirable orchid collection, which we shot in her verdant greenhouse. Ceramicist and artist Samantha McIntyre lives in a truly unique space, complete with a sprawling inner-city rooftop garden. Her affinity with bees plays into her relationship with nature and the art she makes.

Now more than ever it is important that we pay respect to our flora and appreciate its key role in keeping our planet alive. With this book we hope to inspire you to start or expand a flowering indoor or balcony garden of your very own, get closer to nature in your everyday life, and be seduced by the magical world of flowering plants.

SOPHIA AND LAUREN HAVE LONG BELIEVED THAT LIFE IS BETTER SURROUNDED BY FOLIAGE AND FLOWERS

the science of flowers

Flowering plants, referred to collectively as 'angiosperms', make up the vast majority of plants found on Earth. A flower is, at its simplest, the mechanism for a plant's reproduction. The term angiosperm is derived from the Greek *angeion* and *sperma*, and roughly translates to 'seed vessel'. A plant's sexual reproductive organs are contained in the flower. When the plant is fertilised (through cross-pollination or self-pollination), fruit is formed. The fruit contains the seeds that will produce the next generation of plants.

anatomy of a flower

An intricate, interconnecting series of components ensure that floral species continue to thrive.

STAMEN Usually made up of the anther and filament, this is the male fertilising organ and is the pollen-producing part of a flower.

PETAL An important element of the non-reproductive portion of a flower, these are essentially modified leaves that surround the reproductive parts of the plant. Appearing in a myriad of shapes and colours, they are designed to attract insects and other creatures that can facilitate pollination. Collectively known as the corolla.

PISTIL Centrally located and consisting of three main parts (ovary, style and stigma), this is the female reproductive structure of a flower and is primarily designed for the process of pollination. The mature ovary becomes the fruit.

OVULE Located within the ovary, this structure becomes the seeds after fertilisation.

RECEPTACLE The swollen end of the pedicel or flower stalk.

SEPALS Leaf-like in appearance and usually green, these encase and protect the developing bud and go on to support the petals in bloom. Collectively known as the calyx.

PEDUNCLE This is essentially the stalk of a flower or inflorescence. Once pollinated, it will eventually support the fruit as it forms.

pollination

Pollination refers to the transfer of pollen from the female reproductive organs of a plant to the male organs. It is a vital part of the process of seed production and essential for the survival of species.

BEES, ONE OF THE MOST COMMON POLLINATORS, BUZZ AROUND TRANSFERRING POLLEN FROM ONE FLOWER TO THE NEXT

There are two types of pollination in nature: self-pollination and cross-pollination. Self-pollination is the transfer of pollen grains from the male reproductive organ to either the female organ of the same flower or a different flower on the same plant. Cross-pollination occurs when pollen is transferred from one plant to another. Cross-pollination is aided by helpful insects, birds and even bats and other small mammals. Drawn to the beauty and scent of flowers, these creatures will land on or nestle into them to drink their nectar or make a meal of pollen, covering themselves in pollen grains before moving on and distributing the pollen to other plants. Bees are especially important pollinators because they collect pollen for their young and, in doing so, transfer vast amounts among plants. Rain and wind, which can loosen and carry pollen, also contribute to pollination.

Nature is highly intelligent, and many flowers have evolved designs to attract only certain pollinators or developed unique methods of pollen transfer. The broad-lipped bird orchid (*Chiloglottis trapeziformis*) and large bird orchid (*C. valida*) have both developed to look like and produce a scent similar to that of the female wasp. This tricks the male wasp into attempting to mate with the flower, leaving the wasp heavily covered in pollen grains. While the trigger flower (*Stylidium lineare*) has a mechanism that is set off when a potential pollinator lands on its flower, smacking the insect with a wad of pollen grains.

While providing food for pollinators is always a worthy venture, encouraging pollination in your own indoor or balcony garden is only essential if you're hoping for your plants to bear fruit or seeds. If you do wish to aid the process outdoors, the greater the diversity of flowers, the greater the variety of pollinators you will attract to your garden. This is less likely indoors, so try placing your flowering plants on windowsills with the windows open so that bees and other insects can still access them.

If natural pollinators are scarce, or you're hoping to create hybrids of particular plants, hand pollination is the trick. For 'perfect flowers' (those with both male and female reproductive organs), you can simply tap the flower repeatedly to encourage the pollen to transfer from stamen to pistil. For 'imperfect flowers' (those with just male or female reproductive organs), or if you're trying to crossbreed, simply use a delicate artist's brush to collect pollen grains from a mature anther and transfer them to the mature stigma of another flower.

the science of flowers

A VIBRANT *HYDRANGEA MACROPHYLLA* 'PINK'

gardening glossary

AGGREGATE FRUIT A fruit that grows from several ovaries all fused together, like raspberries or blackberries.

ANNUAL A plant that dies once its full life cycle is completed, usually within a single growing season. They need to be replanted every year, or allowed to self-seed.

ANTHER A structure within the stamen that helps to produce and distribute pollen.

BRACT A modified leaf growing from beneath a flower or inflorescence. Bracts are often mistaken for petals as they differ from the foliage leaves in shape, size and colour and help to attract insects for pollination.

CULTIVAR A plant that has been selectively cultivated by humans.

DEADHEADING A technique that involves removing spent flowers to keep a plant looking tidy and help direct its energy into the production of more blooms.

DECIDUOUS A plant that sheds its leaves, usually over the cooler months, regrowing when more desirable conditions return.

DORMANCY A period of rest a plant may enter to conserve energy or to protect itself against undesirable conditions.

DROUGHT-HARDY A plant that can tolerate extended periods without water.

EPIPHYTE A plant that grows on other plants or objects (usually trees), without the need for soil. They are generally non-parasitic to their host. Semi-epiphytic plants live this way for part of their lives.

ETIOLATED A plant that is leggy, weak and pale or yellowing, and may have reduced leaf size and very long internodes, usually caused by a lack of light.

EVERGREEN A plant that maintains its foliage all year and does not lose its leaves.

FAMILY A collection of plants that are grouped according to common genetic ancestors. In taxonomy, a family sits above genus and species, but below kingdom, class and order, and is written with an initial capital letter.

FILAMENT A tube-like structure within the stamen that supports the anther.

FROST HARDY A plant that can survive freezing temperatures; sometimes referred to as 'winter hardy'.

GENUS (PL. GENERA) A group of plants that share the same general characteristics. In taxonomy, a genus sits below family and above species and is written in italics, with an initial capital letter (e.g. *Camellia*).

HABIT A plant's general structure and appearance (e.g. trailing or upright).

HERBACEOUS A vascular plant with no persistent woody stems above ground, including many perennials, annuals, biennials, ferns and graminoids (grasses).

HYBRID The result of cross-pollinating two species of plants within the same genus. Hybridisation can also occur naturally in the wild. All plants can be used to make hybrids, including varieties, cultivars and other hybrids.

INFLORESCENCE A cluster of flowers arranged on a stem; may consist of single or multiple branches.

NYCTINASTY The movement of flowers or leaves triggered by nightly changes in light or temperature.

OVARY The swollen basal section on the pistil that contains ovules or undeveloped seeds.

OVERWINTERING Protecting plants from harsh winter conditions by bringing them indoors or into a more temperate environment. Depending on the plant, this might mean moving them to a sunroom or warm greenhouse, or a cool, dark room.

PERENNIAL A plant that generally lives for more than one year and will continue to bloom year after year with the right conditions once mature. Perennials often have shorter flowering periods than annuals.

PINCHING BACK Cutting back a flush of growth with sharp secateurs just above a leaf node to encourage multiple stems to grow in its place. This should also help to create longer stems and more flowers.

PSEUDOBULB An above-ground, bulb-like structure that grows as part of the stem and helps plants store water and nutrients. Some are quite swollen and very obvious, while others tend to blend in with the leaves that grow from them.

PUPS Also referred to as 'offshoots', these are exact clones of the parent plant produced as a method of self-propagation.

RHIZOME An underground creeping stem that produces both shoots and roots.

SPADIX A type of inflorescence with lots of small flowers borne on a fleshy stem. Very typical of the family Araceae, they are often surrounded by a spathe (leaf-like curved bract).

SPECIES AFFINIS (SP. AFF.) A term used in binomial nomenclature when the identity of a biological species is uncertain but it has a striking similarity or affinity with a known species.

STIGMA Part of the pistil; the pollen-receptive tip of the style, where germination occurs.

STYLE A stalk connecting the ovary and stigma within the pistil.

SUBSPECIES (SUBSP.) A taxonomic grouping within a species used to identify plants that are geographically disparate from one another, with small differences in features.

SYNONYM (SYN.) The previous name of a species that is no longer accepted after further research or genetic testing (e.g. *Senecio radicans* is a synonym for *Curio radicans*).

TEMPERATE A region with mild temperatures; generally devoid of extremes.

TROPICAL A region with warm and humid temperatures; generally frost-free.

UMBEL A type of flower structure where a cluster of blooms all appear on stalks that are nearly equal in length and grow from a central point (e.g. Queen Anne's lace and fennel flowers).

VELUTINOUS Having a fine covering of hairs resulting in a soft, velvety feeling.

RIGHT: SOME THERAPEUTIC AND BEAUTIFUL *ECHINACEA*

flowering plant care

Getting the care of your flowering plants right is the key to encouraging them to fulfil their potential – flourishing and, hopefully, blossoming. Unlike plants in the wild, house plants are almost entirely dependent on us for their needs. A gentle rhythm of learning, potting, positioning, checking in, watering, fertilising, pruning, experimenting and making the occasional mistake will help ensure your garden thrives in your care.

light

Light is non-negotiable when it comes to nurturing our gardens, indoors and out. Through the process of photosynthesis, plants convert sunlight (along with water and carbon dioxide) into energy, which allows them to grow.

Quite simply, plants need light to survive. And while there are some great leafy plant options that will tolerate low-light conditions (like devil's ivy and peace lilies), most plants will require a generous dose of light in order to produce healthy foliage and grow their hugely energy-consuming flowers. Understanding how much light is required is crucial to keeping your plants happy and encouraging those desired blooms in flowering varieties.

The light available to your indoor plants varies hugely. Even on a protected balcony, a plant will probably receive much more sun than it would indoors. Some of the plants we have profiled in this book are only likely to thrive outdoors, while others will happily bear blooms indoors, as long as they're close to a window or skylight.

Our key lists five different types of light options: filtered and direct for indoor dwellers and full shade, part shade and full sun for those living outside.

FILTERED A spot indoors with access to plenty of bright light throughout the day. Plants that thrive in a filtered position will enjoy some direct gentle morning sun but should be sheltered from harsher afternoon rays that will burn their foliage.

DIRECT The brightest light indoors will be close to a natural light source such as a window or skylight with an unobstructed view of the sky. Plants that require this level of light will need access to four to six hours of direct sunlight each day, ideally spread across both morning and afternoon.

FULL SHADE A spot with lots of ambient light, but very little to no direct sun. Plants with sensitive leaves and blooms that will burn if exposed to direct rays will enjoy this position.

PART SHADE A dappled spot or one with sunny and shaded intervals throughout the day. Outdoors, this position would have up to three hours a day in direct sun, with protection from the harshest afternoon sun.

FULL SUN An outdoor or balcony spot that gets six to nine hours of direct sun. Desert-dwelling cacti and succulents, as well as many edibles, are among the plants that need these high levels of direct sun to thrive.

position

Choosing the right spot for your plant is both an aesthetic consideration and a practical one. It will impact the plant's ability to thrive and reward you with flowers. Indoors or out, most plants need a solid amount of sunlight to produce the energy required to bloom. But light isn't the only consideration. Other environmental conditions, like wind, temperature and humidity, along with pest management, choosing the right pots and growth habits, all come into play.

When deciding whether your plant is best suited to a life indoors or out, light is the most important factor. Most common 'indoor' plants are those found natively under the canopies of tropical rainforests in gentle, dappled light. Most succulents, on the other hand, require a lot more direct sun in order to survive and thrive. Just about all plants require a good amount of sunlight to bloom, and many of the plants profiled in this book will not flower unless they are given at least a few hours of direct sun.

Indoors, we can control the environment to a certain degree, but conditions are far more varied outdoors. Balconies, even those that are protected from the elements, generally expose your plants to extreme conditions, from strong direct rays (that some plants will love, but others will despise), to more dramatic rises and dips in temperature. How much these temperature changes impact your plants will depend on where you are located. The relatively temperate conditions of Sydney's cooler months differ vastly from the sub-zero winters experienced in New York. And while some plants will tolerate frost, and may even benefit from it, others will meet an untimely end if exposed to such extremes.

Overwintering, or bringing plants inside or to a more protected environment to avoid frosts, is a great tool for colder climates. Likewise, if your balcony becomes exceedingly hot and sundrenched over summer, a well-placed awning, or repositioning your plants inside, can help more sensitive specimens stay alive. Wind, which can damage plants and expedite potting mix drying out, can be minimised by erecting a screen or planting taller, hardier plants to provide a barrier for more sensitive plants. Indoors, plants can be negatively impacted by air-conditioning units and heaters. Most tropical plants enjoy a more humid environment that can be achieved through regular spritzing or by sitting them on a water-filled pebble tray or near a humidifier, especially during the drier months.

Pests like birds and snails that can't access your indoor plants can be an issue for balcony gardens. Use tricks like bamboo cloches to keep birds away and natural pest control, like beer traps (fill a shallow bowl with beer and dig it so it's level with the soil), to do away with unwanted snails and slugs. Be respectful of this wildlife, and the broader environment, by avoiding toxic pesticides. All insects, especially bees, are precious and important friends

to flowers. On the flip side, your indoor plants are unlikely to be exposed to pollinators – an issue if you're hoping your plant will bear fruit. Our pollination section on pages 16–17 offers some helpful insights.

If you live in an apartment, it's always worth checking if your building has any rules about balcony gardens. There may be weight limits or regulations around saucers to ensure the safety and general wellbeing of your neighbours below. Choose lightweight pots (avoid concrete and ceramics when it comes to larger plants) and fill the base of the pot with an empty, upside-down plastic nursery pot, or natural fillers like pine cones or sticks, to reduce the overall weight of the potted plant. Make sure you leave enough space for the plant's roots to grow.

Our key tells you if a plant is likely to be happiest indoors or out, or if it will make a happy home in either position. Use this position guide and the light requirements to work out the best spot for your plant.

flowering plant care

water

Like light, water is an essential ingredient in the recipe for plant growth. Water makes up about 95 per cent of a plant's tissue. This liquid gold is absorbed mainly through their roots and is responsible for supporting the plant's cell structure, allowing them to be both strong and flexible enough to withstand the elements.

Water also helps to carry important nutrients that aid in growth and reproduction to the stems, leaves and blooms. To help it absorb water, most plants need a well-draining and aerated medium that allows water to flow freely and be taken up into the roots, and for excess to drain away. Some plants require a much moister or more desert-like environment. The potting mix and watering schedule must be tailored to the right conditions.

In the wild, plants receive all the moisture they need from nature, but indoors and on covered balconies they largely rely on us to provide it. No pressure! The most helpful tool for keeping your potting mix the right level of moist is your finger. Dip your digit into the potting mix to judge how much it has dried out and assess whether you need to water again or hold off. There's no one-size-fits-all approach to watering – you need to check the individual requirements of your plant. But on average, most plants need 2–5 cm (¾–2 in) of potting mix to dry out between drinks. One of the biggest plant killers is overwatering – it's hard to come back from root rot – so it's usually better to err on the side of caution and wait a day or two before watering if you're unsure. Always water your plants deeply, but be sure to remove any excess water from the pot's saucer so they aren't sitting in soggy soil.

While some plants may require watering multiple times a week, others will only need a drink every month or so. Bear in mind that your plant's position will impact its water requirements. Those planted outside, exposed to more sun and wind, will dry out faster and will be more likely to evaporate water through their leaves to help them regulate temperature (a process known as transpiration). Pot size and factors like air-conditioning will also impact how quickly potting mix dries out. As the seasons change, you may need to adjust your watering schedule. Use our key as a guide, but be sure to check in regularly with your plants too.

LOW Roughly once every few weeks. Desert-dwelling plants with succulent, water-storing leaves will generally only need to be watered once most of the potting mix has dried out.

MODERATE Roughly once a week, depending on the external factors mentioned above. Most of the plants profiled in this book will fall somewhere around this point, requiring watering once the top 2–5 cm (¾–2 in) of potting mix has dried out.

HIGH Two or three times a week. Moisture-loving plants will need to be watered once the surface of the potting mix has dried out.

potting mix

This innocuous seeming dirt is mostly out of sight, but don't let it be out of mind. It plays an incredibly important role in a plant's health and vitality, providing support for root growth, and facilitating the passing of water, oxygen and nutrients into the plant.

The importance of soil health to our ecosystem is becoming increasingly clear. Just one teaspoon of healthy soil can contain anywhere between two billion and seven billion microbes, all of which help to capture carbon, decompose organic matter and spur plant growth. For indoor or balcony gardens, the quality of the potting medium the plants grow in will directly impact their strength and resilience.

The difference between soil and potting mix is that soil is naturally occurring, while potting mix is an intentional concoction of various ingredients. These ingredients include a combination of organic animal or plant-based materials like compost and manure, inorganic natural additions to aid aeration, fertiliser and optional extras like pH-balancing lime, beneficial microbes and wetting agents, depending on the type.

Different groups of plants benefit from varying types of potting medium. Where possible, try to use a potting mix that is most specific to the plant you are growing. Succulents and cacti require a drier, coarser, very well draining mix, but leafy tropical plants tend to need a base that retains some moisture while allowing excess water to flow away to avoid waterlogging and the eventual suffocation of a plant's roots. Most of the common indoor plants will thrive in a good-quality general house-plant mix. There are, of course, some exceptions, for example, epiphytic orchids that grow on trees in rainforests prefer a soil-free mix containing bark chips, and maybe the addition of charcoal or perlite to help with drainage. This very loose mix will also work well for bromeliads and other epiphytes. Acid-loving plants like camellias, roses, gardenias, azaleas, blueberries and rhododendrons will benefit from a specific mix, often sold as a 'camellia and rose' potting mix.

Generally, the more expensive the store-bought potting mix, the better the quality – and it's something we recommend investing in. Be sure to choose one that is free of peat moss, which is a wholly unsustainable ingredient. Opt instead for the more environmentally friendly coco or coir peat (made from widely available coconut fibre).

Creating your own compost or castings is a fantastic way to add nutrients and microdiversity to your potting mix. Although not everyone has the space for a big compost pile, even a small balcony can accommodate a compact worm farm. These nifty contraptions can house hundreds of worms who work tirelessly to digest organic food waste and turn it into nutrient-

dense castings and worm wee. Bokashi composting systems are also a great compact option. With food waste being one of the most dangerous contributors to the climate crisis, you could kill two birds with one stone and feed your edible waste to the worms or compost and they will both repay you with liquid gold for your plants. When potting a new plant, it is best to use a thoroughly cleaned pot filled with fresh potting mix to decrease the chance of transferring any sneaky pests or diseases. We recommend that pots have drainage holes at the base to allow you to water deeply and ensure any excess moisture can escape. For planters without drainage, double potting is the best option: simply keep your plant in its plastic nursery pot which was multiple drainage holes in the base, and sit this inside an outer, more attractive pot, known as a cache pot.

Our key lists three general types of potting mix: well draining, moisture retaining, and coarse + sandy. Sometimes we list a combination of the three, or state if there is a plant-specific potting mix available.

flowering plant care

fertiliser

Fertiliser can play a vital role in encouraging robust foliage growth and is even more important for supporting blooms in flowering plants. To carry out the essential process of photosynthesis, plants need at least 16 elements. While carbon, oxygen and hydrogen are acquired from air and water, the nitrogen, magnesium and iron that, in their natural habitat, would be readily accessible from the soil, must be provided to plants in containers by us.

Fresh potting mix is generally enhanced with slow-release fertiliser, but as time goes on, those nutrients are either absorbed by the plant or leached from the soil through watering. Without these essential elements plants can become weakened and experience slowed growth and reduced flowering. That's where fertiliser comes in.

Fertilising plants is most important during their active growing periods. This is generally in the warmer months of spring and summer, but is really any time that a plant is producing regular growth or during their flowering period. Some of the signs that a plant would benefit from a feed include leaf drop, yellowing lower leaves and slowed or no growth. On the flip side, when plants enter a period of dormancy, they use much less energy and will not require any fertiliser top-ups. Over-fertilising a plant during any period, but especially during this time, can result in wilting, burnt leaf tips, yellow leaves and potentially the plant's demise. Err on the side of caution by diluting the fertiliser to one-half or even one-quarter of what is recommended in the product instructions. You can always add more if needed but it's much harder to come back from applying too much.

All plant fertilisers are made up of a combination of macro and micronutrients derived either chemically or organically. As with potting mix, we suggest opting for a good-quality organic fertiliser. They improve the health of the potting mix and can be applied less frequently, which reduces the risk of overdoing it.

Fertiliser is available in a variety of forms. The most common are liquid and granular (slow-release) fertiliser. Diluted in water and applied directly to the potting mix, liquid fertiliser can be added as part of your watering regime. Depending on the type of plant, a fortnightly or monthly application is ideal. In liquid form, fertiliser is quickly and easily absorbed but doesn't last as long as the granular form. Sprinkled on top of the soil, granular fertiliser releases nutrients slowly over time, which means you won't see results as quickly. However, it also means the plants need to be fed far less regularly – perfect for the busy gardener. When adding granular fertiliser, be sure to loosen the soil with a fork or spade and water deeply to activate.

maintenance

General maintenance, including pruning, goes a long way to keeping our plants happy and healthy. Let's face it, we all feel a million dollars after a good haircut and house plants are no different. Checking in regularly, keeping leaves clean and dust-free and removing dead leaf matter will help stave off pests and disease, which can strike when a plant is vulnerable.

Indoor plants will benefit greatly from a fortnightly wiping down of their leaves with a damp cloth or a soft goat's hair brush. A monthly rinse under the shower will help remove stubborn dust and has the added benefit of giving plants a deep drink. Outdoors, make sure that your plants aren't sitting in stagnant water and empty their saucers regularly if rain can fill them up.

Adhering to a regular plant maintenance routine means you are best placed to notice any issues before they become established. While watering your plants, look for pests that might be lurking. They tend to hide out in tiny nooks and crannies, so be thorough. If you find anything of concern, quarantine the affected plant from the rest of your gang to avoid pests spreading while you deal with the issue.

While it may sometimes feel that you're gardening solely for the benefit of the local wildlife, remember that they are an important part of the ecosystem. Before they become beautiful butterflies, caterpillars need to feed on leaves. Possums and squirrels might be collecting food for their babies, and aphids provide important sustenance for lady beetles.

You can rehome caterpillars and snails or catch them in beer traps. Some gardeners also swear by copper tape, which can be stuck in a loop around containers to act as a barrier. For smaller pests like aphids and scale, wipe down leaves with soapy water to carefully remove as many as you can before applying an eco oil or diluted vegetable oil that should suffocate most of the remaining bugs. Repeat weekly to disrupt their life cycle and ensure no pests remain. Recently, we have been making use of sacrificial plants outdoors – allowing aphids to take over one yummy plant, in the hope that they leave the others alone. Always try to avoid toxic pesticides, as they can kill helpful pollinators and leach into our water systems.

Pruning can play an important role in creating fullness in foliage. Likewise, deadheading or removing spent flowers can prolong the blooming period by allowing plants to redirect energy from seed production into new flower growth. Be sure to use a clean, sharp pair of secateurs, and cut at the base of the stem. Some plants can even have their dead leaves or flowers removed by twisting and either pulling or pushing. This helps create a clean break and lessens the chance of the plant suffering a post-op infection.

cut flowers

While we love enjoying the beauty of our flowers on the plant from which they have grown, there's also a distinct pleasure in being able to cut from your own indoor or balcony garden to create a little posy in a vase. This will have the added benefit of allowing your plant to put more energy into subsequent flower production and stimulate strong foliage growth.

The way you remove and prepare the flowers can increase their life span in a vase. Here are some simple tips to keep your cuttings fresh for longer.

- Always cut stems using sharp, clean secateurs.

- Cut outdoor plants in the cooler mornings rather than in the middle of the day.

- Cut from the base of the stem so you don't leave unsightly bare stems that may also cause rot issues.

- Make sure the vessel you use is sparklingly clean.

- Fill your vessel generously with room-temperature water.

- Remove any leaves that fall below the water line.

- Recut stems and plunge quickly into water.

- Refresh vase water every day or so, and take this opportunity to recut the stems to allow water to continue to travel upwards.

A big bounty of flowers looks great casually dropped into a large vase. Make sure there is variety in the length of stems. When it comes to vases, we love handmade ceramics and heavy glass vessels. If you have just a couple of special specimens, bud vases are a great way to let the flowers shine. Experiment, and let your creativity reign.

And, once they've passed their prime, be sure to dispose of flowers mindfully, putting them in the compost or green bin.

a year of flowering plants

Plants devote considerable resources and energy into producing flowers, so it makes sense that they correlate their efforts with a time of year when conditions are ideal for reproductive success. From spring, when nature appears to burst back to life after a period of hibernation, through the intense heat of summer, the more restful but still resplendent autumn, and finally the quieter, calmer months of winter, there are a huge range of flowering plants to be enjoyed as each season progresses.

While many plants will bloom over multiple seasons, we have grouped our profiles into chapters based on when their flowers are at their peak.

For some profiles we have explored specific species, while for others we have featured the genus more generally.

Use these profiles as a guide to create a garden, indoors or out, that will bring endless floral joy. Let them be a starting point for your own exploration of the plants that catch your eye.

key

Light filtered (gentle direct morning, indirect afternoon)/direct (lots of direct sun through a window)/full shade (outdoor, away from direct sun)/part shade (dappled or intermittent outdoor sunlight)/full sun (six to nine hours direct)

Water low (about once a month)/ moderate (about once a week)/ high (about two to three times a week)

Soil well draining/moisture retaining/ coarse + sandy/species specific

Position indoor/balcony

Frost hardy yes/no

Expert level novice/green thumb/expert

A time of abundance, spring is a riot of colour, texture and scent. Bulbs burst forth and small trees drip with blooms. As the temperature rises and the days get longer, shower your plants with attention – repot them, fertilise regularly and set up an attentive watering schedule. Then sit back and enjoy the vibrant results.

spring

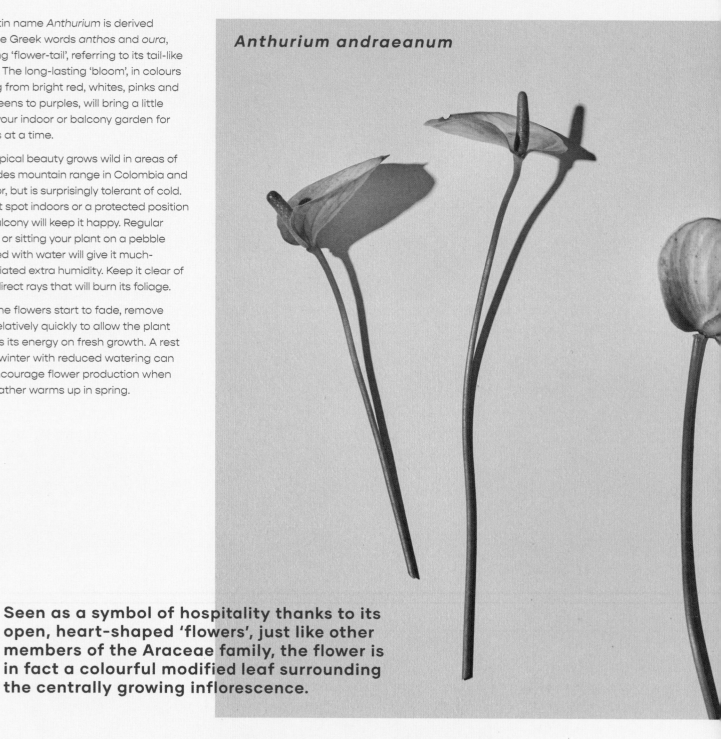

Anthurium andraeanum

The Latin name *Anthurium* is derived from the Greek words *anthos* and *oura*, meaning 'flower-tail', referring to its tail-like spadix. The long-lasting 'bloom', in colours ranging from bright red, whites, pinks and light greens to purples, will bring a little fun to your indoor or balcony garden for months at a time.

This tropical beauty grows wild in areas of the Andes mountain range in Colombia and Ecuador, but is surprisingly tolerant of cold. A bright spot indoors or a protected position on a balcony will keep it happy. Regular misting or sitting your plant on a pebble tray filled with water will give it much-appreciated extra humidity. Keep it clear of harsh direct rays that will burn its foliage.

Once the flowers start to fade, remove them relatively quickly to allow the plant to focus its energy on fresh growth. A rest during winter with reduced watering can help encourage flower production when the weather warms up in spring.

Seen as a symbol of hospitality thanks to its open, heart-shaped 'flowers', just like other members of the Araceae family, the flower is in fact a colourful modified leaf surrounding the centrally growing inflorescence.

Flamingo flower

FLOWERS spring to summer, sometimes year round
FAMILY Araceae
LIGHT filtered/part shade to full shade
WATER moderate
SOIL well draining
POSITION indoor/balcony
FROST HARDY no
EXPERT LEVEL novice

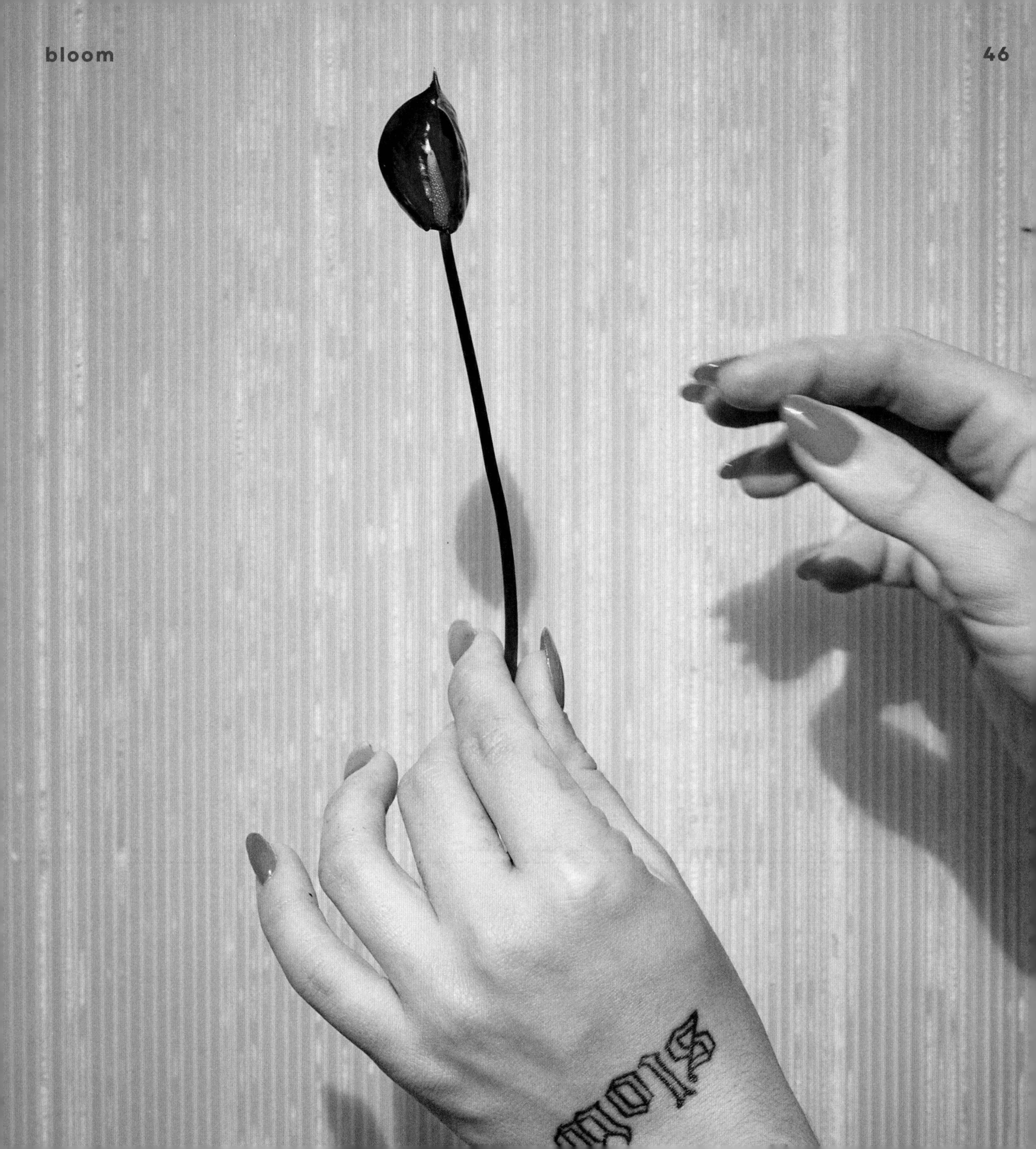

FLOWERS spring to autumn
FAMILY Araceae
LIGHT filtered
WATER moderate
SOIL well draining
POSITION indoor
FROST HARDY no
EXPERT LEVEL novice

SPATHIPHYLLUM WALLISII IN AN ASOBIMASU CLAY PLANTER

Peace lily

When we think of indoor flowering plants, the humble peace lily is probably one of the first that springs to mind. Producing elegant white flowers that pop against its rich green foliage through much of the year, this classic indoor plant needs minimal amounts of TLC to thrive.

Spathiphyllum

Sometimes referred to as the 'closet plant' for its ability to tolerate lower light conditions, *Spathiphyllum* will survive in a darker position but are unlikely to bloom in such a spot. A position with plenty of bright, indirect light is your best bet to allow this lush bloomer to live its best life.

As with all members of the Araceae family, the flowers of *Spathiphyllum* are borne on a type of inflorescence known as a spadix. What many assume to be the flower of the peace lily is in fact a specialised leaf bract or spath that surrounds the inflorescence.

It's worth noting that *Spathiphyllum* will only start producing blooms once it reaches maturity, which can take up to a year. Many plants on the market, although in bloom, are still in their juvenile state. Commercial growers coax younger plants to flower for saleability by adding gibberellic acid – a naturally occurring hormone that stimulates cell division and can promote flowering and fruiting.

Once the plant matures, a well-draining potting medium and a regular feed with organic liquid fertiliser through spring and summer will stand you in good stead for achieving those desired flowers. Thankfully, the stunning ribbed foliage should keep you satisfied while you wait.

The humble cornflower has been cultivated in attractive burgundy, red, pink, white and purple colourings in addition to the distinct cornflower blue for which it is best known. Historically it grew as a weed but, despite these modest beginnings, it is a favourite of ours for floral arrangements. Whether in a vase or potted close together, the flowers look great among other field flowers like poppies, cosmos, rudbeckia, tickseed, California poppy and echinacea. The brightly coloured edible petals also look great scattered over cakes or ice-cream.

Cornflowers can grow tall, up to 90 cm (3 ft), and may require staking to help support their weak stems. They can handle drier potting mix once established, but regular watering will help to produce a strong flowering. Deadhead regularly, but towards the end of the growing season you may want to let some blooms go to seed, either to save for the garden (so they can self-sow or for you to collect and plant again next spring) or to let the birds enjoy a little treat.

Centaurea cyanus

Centaurea cyanus, **commonly referred to as cornflower as it is often found growing in corn and other grain fields, produces a flutter of delicate petals most often in striking royal blue.**

Cornflower

FLOWERS late spring
to early autumn
FAMILY Asteraceae
LIGHT full sun
WATER moderate
SOIL moisture
retaining/well draining
POSITION balcony
FROST HARDY yes
EXPERT LEVEL novice

FLOWERS spring to autumn
FAMILY Asteraceae
LIGHT full sun
WATER moderate
SOIL well draining
POSITION balcony
FROST HARDY no
EXPERT LEVEL novice

COSMOS ATROSANGUINEUS

Cosmos

One of the easiest annuals to grow, *Cosmos* comes in a myriad of colours and styles. Our favourites include the heavenly scented 'chocolate cosmos' (*C. atrosanguineus*) with its deep burgundy, velutinous flowers, and the prettiest, fluffiest 'cupcake blush' (*C. bipinnatus*). Despite their delicious names, it's worth noting that these plants are toxic.

Cosmos

Cosmos is often grown from small seedlings or seeds (check out Floret Flowers for the most amazing cultivars if you are from the US or Canada). Plant them out in early spring once the chance of frost has passed. They grow fast and benefit from pinching back (cutting just above a leaf node to encourage multiple stems to grow in its place), which should encourage longer stems and more flowers. Pinched back or not, they have a wild vibe and may need to be staked or alternatively potted between supporting plants. If space is at a premium, keep an eye out for dwarf varieties.

The more you cut the flowers from this gratifying plant, the more it will produce, so either deadhead once flowers are spent or cut as the flower is beginning to bloom and pop in a vase. Fertilise once a month during the growing season. Prune back and bring your plants inside over winter (if you're in a colder climate) to ensure they don't get destroyed by frost.

slow flowers / Petrina Burrill

Petrina Burrill is a passionate slow gardener who has been designing flower gardens for years. Also a florist, she creates beautiful, handpicked bouquets from her own garden.

For Petrina, gardening brings true happiness and is a wonderful passion to bring joy in life. Her Instagram page @petrinablooms (well worth a follow) charts her seasonal adventures with flowers and her infectious, happy zest for life.

WHEN DID YOU DISCOVER YOUR LOVE OF PLANTS?

My first memory of plants and a garden is being four years old and walking through my great-grandmother's garden beds of delphinium and columbines. I clearly remember peering up to the sky with flowers all around me. There were butterflies, the scent of garden roses... I thought I'd entered a magical land. Her son went on to maintain the shire gardens in Mathoura (country NSW), and he in turn passed the love of gardening on to my mum. There was always a small vase of flowers on the table for each meal or plant cuttings growing in vases of water. Mum was always drowning her indoor plants in her teapot leaves. She taught us to love nature from a very young age. In my Year 6 diary I wrote, 'When I grow up, I want to be a florist or a gardener.' We always had a house full of plants and flowers.

ABOVE: FRESH CUT POPPIES   RIGHT: PETRINA IN HER ELEMENT, COLLECTING ROSES IN HER LUSH, FLOWER-FILLED GARDEN

HOW LONG HAVE YOU BEEN CREATING YOUR CURRENT GARDEN?

My current garden has been a work in progress for ten years. A hidden, floral oasis in the inner city that bursts with colour and joy. Each autumn I plant around 8000 bulbs and corms. I have a 50-year-old wisteria-covered outdoor room that I use for my floral workshop. It shares the pergola with a Virginia creeper – they get on really well. I love collecting roses, especially David Austin's. I have more than 120 rose bushes – my friends often enquire how Flemington Racecourse is going. The boundary is surrounded with established trees, my favourite being a 30-year-old *Gleditsia* 'Sunburst'. Her branches gracefully fall to meet the ground. Pull them back and you enter another green room.

My next project is to add to my 'room' of cherry blossoms in wine barrels that surround my deck. I have four but I want to be enclosed by them, so I will add more barrels around the deck boundaries to create a blossom room come spring. I think gardens should be full of their own rooms.

TELL US ABOUT THE CONCEPT OF 'SLOW FLOWERS'.

The slow flower movement is my kind of gardening. It involves no nasties and is the real deal, just as my great-grandmother gardened in her days. Think the opposite of fast flowers – mass-produced, sprayed with synthetic pesticides and herbicides, artificial environments to fast-track growth and flown in plane fridges around the world to reach wholesale markets.

Slow flowers are grown with love, patience and kindness. The movement puts our precious planet first. It's so important to ask where your flowers and plants have come from.

YOU HAVE A REAL KNACK FOR BEAUTY AND ABUNDANCE IN THE GARDEN. WHAT ARE YOUR BEST TIPS FOR GROWING IN CONTAINERS?

Most flowers and plants can be grown in containers. My last house had a small courtyard so I filled pots with tulips and daffodils. Here, I have a huge deck. It is practical, but it

RIGHT: POTS LINE PETRINA'S DECK, FILLED TO THE BRIM WITH HAPPY FLOWERS

was also stark and harsh on the eyes. I softened it with blossom trees and Japanese maple in wine barrels. In springtime it comes to life with a thousand bulbs in smaller pots – tulips, ranunculus, daffodils. Good potting mix, some sunshine, water and air – they all take off and do their own thing. I love watching bulbs wake up just in time for spring. They just know what to do.

AND TO ENCOURAGE THE BEST BLOOMS?

You can add some Seasol if you wish. I try to buy new bulbs each year. The goodness comes ready in the bulb from the farms. I give the old ones away or plant them in community spaces or make random fairy gardens for people to enjoy. Gardening is about the imagination.

My young daughter helps keep our container fairy garden going out the front gate. Little porcelain fairies hide among pots of green and flowers. Children are always stopping.

WHAT ARE YOUR FAVOURITE POTTED FLOWERING PLANTS TO GROW IN EACH SEASON?

In summer I enjoy foxgloves, hollyhocks, gardenias, garden roses and cosmos in my containers. They grow easily from seeds I plant in spring. It's beautiful to watch the bees and dragonflies dance from bloom to bloom.

Autumn is my favourite season in the garden. It's when I work the garden beds and pots sending all my bulbs to sleep. Meanwhile the dahlias, cosmos and amaranthus I planted in November are making a show. They love pots. So do my roses. I love the wonderful colours the autumn roses bring – one last shout out of joy before they sleep for the winter.

In winter I have japonica, early daffodils, daphne and camellias growing in containers. Winter is a very busy time in the garden. I have my open fires burning inside and out, there are always jobs to do. Cut daphne and japonica in vases inside bring me hope of a garden about to burst to life in the weeks to come.

Spring is a riot! Cherry blossoms, fresh maple leaves, tulips, anemones, ranunculus – they fill my deck and garden beds like a carpet. My wisteria steals the show, wrapping her purple shawl from above. A true riot of colour and magic! Everyone is awake and bringing joy.

HOW CAN WE MAKE OUR GARDENS MORE SUSTAINABLE?

Whether it's veggies or flowers, it's great to be self-sufficient. If you grow your own flowers you won't need to buy them again and you're helping the environment in many ways. I always tell people to start small with a few pots and grow what you love – the smallest pot of tulips will lift your spirits and last for weeks indoors.

The gardening community is brilliant at sharing and giving. Many of my plants are cuttings from friends' gardens. A bonus with container gardening is that you can move them into the sun or away to protect them. In many ways, they are easier to care for.

ABOVE: A BASKET OF FRESHLY CUT ROSES ON THE FRONT SEAT OF PETRINA'S 1966 AP6 VALIANT   RIGHT: PETRINA AMONG HER ABUNDANT ROSE BUSHES

LEFT: SEASIDE DAISIES IN A TERRACOTTA POT   CENTRE: FRESHLY CUT ROSES   RIGHT: BUTTONS THE CAT LOVES THE BLOOMS AS MUCH AS PETRINA DOES

"The slow flower movement is my kind of gardening. It involves no nasties and is the real deal, just as my great-grandmother gardened in her days."

WHAT HAS GARDENING TAUGHT YOU ABOUT LIFE?

Gardens are beautiful metaphors for life. Everything must come and go, everything has its time, place and purpose. I love that they are universal and date back thousands of years. They remind us that tomorrow is never promised to us. Flowers and gardens show me how to live in the present and be grateful. They also hold and release memories; they hold time. Lily of the valley takes me back to being five years old in my great-nan's garden on a warm spring day. A fragrant flower is a thing of intense, almost overwhelming beauty.

Gardening is a dreamy pastime; it takes you away. Dreamy, uplifting, ethereal; it's a place where time stops and daydreaming begins. As a traveller I've spent most of my life dreaming of faraway places. As a gardener I've created a space that lets me and others go back to those faraway places through flowers and plants. Gardening also puts life in perspective. It's real, you're in the moment with Mother Nature, Herself. Nothing makes me happier than seeing the joy my garden brings.

AS A FORMER FLIGHT ATTENDANT, YOU MUST HAVE VISITED MANY DIFFERENT PLACES AROUND THE WORLD. WHAT ARE SOME OF THE MOST MAGICAL PLANT-FILLED SPOTS?

During international layovers I would find gardens and florists in each city. I love the Kew Gardens in London and Jardin Majorelle in Marrakech. I became known as the 'Flower Girl' with the customs officers in the United Arab Emirates because I always returned home to Dubai with flowers flowing out the back of my trolley dolly bag. The smell of lilac reminds me of how it grew wild in the streets of Munich – I'd pick armfuls and bring it back for friends. Seeing the dogwoods in flower in Yosemite in May was spellbinding. I'd find peonies growing in back laneways in Zurich and I'll never forget the wildflowers in Crete in April. I have a story for almost every flower from my travels. Flowers are very personal. Almost everyone has a story about what a flower means to them and why.

WALLISIA CYANEA 'VARIEGATED'

Wallisia cyanea

Pink quill plant

Small but mighty is how we describe *Wallisia cyanea* (syn. *Tillandsia cyanea*). Growing to much smaller heights than its bromeliad relatives, what it lacks in stature it most definitely makes up for with its incredibly vibrant bracts and dainty flowers.

FLOWERS spring to summer
FAMILY Bromeliaceae
LIGHT filtered
WATER moderate
SOIL well draining
(or none!)
POSITION indoor
FROST HARDY no
EXPERT LEVEL novice

The showy pink bracts that resemble ink quills are long-lasting, and stay on display for several months. In spring and summer pretty little violet flowers will emerge from the bracts. These will each only survive a few days before dying off.

Pink quill plants will take at least a few years to reach maturity and blooming age but thankfully many are sold at maturity for those of us for whom patience is not a virtue. Ensure the plant receives plenty of bright, indirect light to help bring on the blooms but remember to shield it from direct afternoon sun.

Unlike most other *Wallisia* species, *W. cyanea* will grow happily both in and out of a pot, so you have options for displaying your pink quill. In a pot, opt for a potting mix that is specific for epiphytes. The addition of orchid bark or coco chips can help create a very well draining mix. If choosing the out-of-pot option, hang your pink quill plant or display it in a footed bowl. To water a plant without potting medium, submerge the whole plant in distilled water for an hour before turning it upside down and allowing it to thoroughly drain, ensuring no moisture is left in the central urn of the plant.

This plant is very easy to propagate from offsets, which is a good thing given that, as the bract diminishes, turning from pink to green, the plant will also begin to die off. The pups will form at the base of the mother plant. Once the mother dies off, you can remove the dead foliage or remove the pup completely.

Although it may take four years for your *Echeveria* to produce its first bloom, once it does, it should reward your care with flowers every subsequent year. Many of the original 150 species have been crossed to make over a thousand cultivars, meaning there is a plethora of *Echeveria* to choose from.

Each flower stalk, which grows from close to the centre of the plant, can reach up to 30 cm (12 in). On top of the stalk will be up to 12 clusters of flowers in bright yellows, oranges, whites, pinks or reds. Most *Echeveria* species flower from spring to summer.

Like most other succulents, make sure the top layer of soil is dry before watering again and be sure to avoid watering the rosettes, as this can cause them to rot. Use a succulent-friendly fertiliser when they start flowering to give them a much-needed energy boost. They are very easily propagated by placing a gently removed leaf onto dry potting mix.

Echeveria

Originating in the mountainous areas of Central and South America, this flower-shaped evergreen succulent looks attractive all year round.

Hen and chicks

ECHEVERIA 'BIG RED'

FLOWERS spring to summer
FAMILY Crassulaceae
LIGHT full sun
WATER low to moderate
SOIL coarse + sandy
POSITION balcony
FROST HARDY
species dependent
EXPERT LEVEL novice

spring

FLOWERS spring to autumn
FAMILY Geraniaceae
LIGHT part shade to full sun
WATER moderate
SOIL moisture retaining/
well draining
POSITION balcony
FROST HARDY no
EXPERT LEVEL novice

GERANIUM WALLICHIANUM × HIMALAYENSE 'ROZANNE'

Cranesbill

Geranium is often confused with its sister genus *Pelargonium*. One way of distinguishing the two is to look at their flowers. *Geranium* species have five similar petals radiating from a central point, while *Pelargonium* species have two petals above and three below.

Additionally, *Geranium* usually has smaller, more delicate leaves. *Pelargonium* is commonly referred to as 'geranium', and true geranium as 'hardy' or 'perennial geranium'. As confusing as this all is, once you understand the differences, it will be easy to differentiate between the genera.

Another common name for *Geranium* is the cranesbill, which refers to its seed pods which are reminiscent of the bill of a crane (funnily enough!). Before these pods appear, a flower blooms. Delicate petals appear in spring and continue to provide joy into summer, with some species even lasting until autumn. During the colder months, it may enter a period of dormancy, but most species are winter hardy, so although the foliage may die back, it should spring back to life again when warmer temperatures return.

There are over 400 species of *Geranium* and many cultivars, but we especially love *G. phaeum* 'Springtime' with its deep burgundy blooms and variegated juvenile leaves, *G. pratense* 'Splish splash' with its wildly speckled white and purple flowers, *G. macrorrhizum* 'Ingwersen's variety' with its red buds, pale pink blooms, and fragrant leaves, and *G. wallichianum* × *himalayense* 'Rozanne' (pictured). The bold white centre of these flowers is connected to their bright purple petals with intricate red veins.

Geranium

SINNINGIA BULLATA IN A LEAF AND THREAD POT

Sinningia bullata

Emerald forest

Sporting crinkled, vivid green leaves and the brightest of red-orange flowers, *Sinningia bullata* is a cheery plant indeed. Add to that a woolliness covering the underside of its foliage and newly formed flowers and you have yourself one seriously unique indoor plant.

FLOWERS year round with a peak in spring and summer
FAMILY Gesneriaceae
LIGHT filtered/part shade
WATER moderate
SOIL well draining
POSITION indoor/balcony
FROST HARDY no
EXPERT LEVEL novice

Hailing from the island of Florianópolis off southern Brazil, where it grows in relatively harsh conditions on steep rocky slopes, this hardy plant is a close relative of the African violet. It is adaptable to a range of growing conditions. Tolerant of cooler temperatures, unlike other tuberous *Sinningia*, it doesn't go dormant in winter, producing its lovely foliage and flowers year round.

Low light conditions may result in leggy growth and fewer flowers so opt for a nice bright position. A few hours of direct morning sun, but shielded from harsher afternoon rays, is ideal to encourage blooms without burning those textured leaves. If foliage does get leggy, the plant responds well to a good trim. Simply pinch off any etiolated growth for a bushier plant.

While tolerant of periods of dryness, it will struggle to deal with soggy feet, so less is best when it comes to watering.

Featuring striking foliage in addition to its velvety blooms in a plethora of hues, *Anigozanthos* can take some looking after, but are well worth the effort.

While some varieties will live a happy long life (over 20 years in some cases), others are more short-lived. This variability means that different species and hybrids can have differing care requirements, so it pays to know what you're dealing with to be sure you treat it properly.

Smaller hybrids seem to work best for container planting, as watering is more manageable. It is a common misconception that kangaroo paws prefer dry conditions – while they can tolerate periods of dryness through the colder months, they will struggle to thrive without adequate moisture during active growth. When conditions are particularly warm, regular watering is essential, especially for potted plants whose potting mix can dry out quickly. Adding a layer of pebbles or mulch to the top of the soil can help the plant retain moisture and prevent the potting mix from overheating. A very well draining medium will suit these plants to a tee.

Anigozanthos

As its common name suggests, this Australian native produces furry, tubular flowers that resemble the paw of another Aussie local, the kangaroo.

Kangaroo paw

FLOWERS spring to summer
FAMILY Haemodoraceae
LIGHT full sun
WATER moderate
SOIL coarse + sandy/
well draining
POSITION balcony
FROST HARDY no
EXPERT LEVEL
green thumb

The bold blooms of this flower always make us think of the Dutch masters' paintings that featured them, such as Jan Davidsz de Heem's *Vase of Flowers* and *An Arrangement with Flowers* by Georgius Jacobus Johannes van Os.

Languid stems lead to an endless variety of blooms in a multitude of colours, patterns, shapes and textures. There are over 6000 cultivars, which are generally broken down into 15 groups, including the parrot tulip in all its colourful ruffled splendour, the lily-flowered tulip with its pointy, reflexed petals, the fringed tulip with its frayed petal edge, and the classic single and double flowering plants.

Tulips grow from a bulb and need a bit more specialised treatment than some more common indoor and balcony plants. They are traditionally planted out in autumn, flower in spring, and are then taken out of the soil once they enter their dormant stage and stored in a cool dry spot over the hotter months.

Tulipa

Tulips are steeped in a rich and evocative history. Originating in the mountainous regions of Central Asia, these unusually beautiful plants were first cultivated in Iran before they became immensely popular in Turkey and then the Netherlands. This culminated in 'tulip mania'. For a brief period in the 1630s, during the Dutch Golden Age, rare and special bulbs could fetch the equivalent of the price of a house. The market inevitably crashed, but tulips continue to be a hugely popular flower, loved and grown the world over.

Tulip

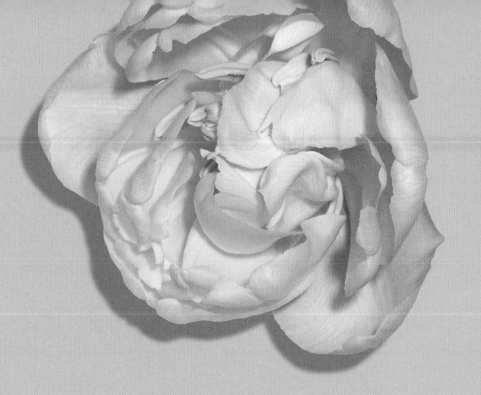

FLOWERS spring
FAMILY Liliaceae
LIGHT full sun
WATER moderate
SOIL well draining
POSITION
indoor/balcony
FROST HARDY yes
EXPERT LEVEL
green thumb

Because tulips have been so excessively bred, some cultivars will be less likely to perform year on year, making them more of an annual. Others don't require so much attention and will happily lie dormant in their pot before emerging again the following spring. It's always worth checking the specific instructions for the species or cultivar you have your hands on.

When planting your bulbs, choose a decent-sized pot and place them quite close together. Tulips en masse is the look to go for. A good rule of thumb is to plant the bulb (pointy end up) about three times as deep as the height of the bulb itself. If you live in a colder climate, you will need to plant your tulip bulbs before temperatures drop too dramatically. Water in and then place the pots in a protected spot (such as an unheated garage) that will expose the bulbs to cool temperatures but save them from freezing. If you find yourself in a warmer environment, you can trick the bulbs by placing them in the crisper of your fridge for six to 12 weeks before planting. Whether naturally occurring or mimicked, this cooling off is vital to ensuring strong growth and flowering. Once spring arrives and the first growth appears above the potting mix, you can move your plants to a sunnier, warmer spot. Your plants should flower for about six weeks. Try to keep them away from excessive heat and humidity.

If you are going down the bulb-storing route, cut the flower stem off once flowering is complete, but always allow the foliage to yellow and die off naturally before removing the bulb from the potting mix. This allows the bulb to sequester valuable nutrients from the rest of the plant, which it needs to flower the following season. Once the plant has died back above the ground, take your bulbs out of the potting mix and give them a quick brush clean before popping in a paper or netted bag. Don't forget to label the bags and store them in a cool, dry place until they're ready to plant out the following autumn.

Appearing in a variety of shades from orange and yellow through to lilac and pink, *Abutilon* can flower in abundance from spring until autumn, so you get plenty of bang for your buck.

In addition to its fabulous flowers, the maple-like foliage of *Abutilon* is beautiful and evergreen, ensuring year-round appeal. Water frequently in summer, keeping the rich, well-draining potting mix consistently moist, but back off in the cooler months. A full-sun or part-shade position shielded from the elements is best but note that direct rays will encourage more abundant flowering.

For optimal plant health, an annual feed in spring with slow-release fertiliser, topped up during the flowering season with a monthly dose of liquid fertiliser, will be appreciated. It can reach heights of around 2 m (6½ ft), but there are also several dwarf forms (like that pictured here) that are wonderfully compact and ideal for courtyards and balconies.

Abutilon

Closely related to hibiscus, *Abutilon* or Chinese lanterns are so named for their distinct lantern-like blooms that hang pendulously on this fast-growing shrub.

Chinese lantern

FLOWERS spring to autumn
FAMILY Malvaceae
LIGHT part shade/full sun
WATER moderate to high
SOIL well draining
POSITION balcony
FROST HARDY no
EXPERT LEVEL novice

MEDINILLA DOLICHOPHYLLA × ALATA

Giant chandelier plant

Revered as an exotic house plant for hundreds of years, *Medinilla* has a mildly broad range across the tropical regions of Africa, Madagascar, South-East Asia, western Pacific Islands and Australia.

FLOWERS spring to summer
FAMILY Melastomataceae
LIGHT filtered/part shade
WATER moderate to high
SOIL well draining
POSITION indoor/balcony
FROST HARDY no
EXPERT LEVEL expert

Medinilla grows epiphytically in the fork of large trees but can equally make a happy home indoors or on a protected balcony.

This magnificent, tropical plant sports leathery leaves with cascading flowers that can reach up to 45 cm (18 in) in length. The drooping clusters of small, pastel pink, white, purple or coral red flowers appear in late spring and resemble a bunch of grapes. Some varieties feature delicate bracts at the base of their flower clusters that look like petals. It is a particularly spectacular flower to behold.

Medinilla is happiest in warm humid conditions. Indoors, bright filtered light is best and outside it enjoys dappled light and shelter from harsh afternoon sun. Keep the well-draining soil moist by watering deeply at least once a week and keep humidity high with daily misting of the leaves, while avoiding the flowers. When the stunning blooms are spent, be sure to remove them to prolong the plant's flowering period.

After flowering, give the plant orchid-specific or regular fertiliser and prune back unwanted branches to promote new growth. You can cut it back almost to base level but be sure to leave at least one leaf set on each stalk so it doesn't die back completely. Although *Medinilla* can be a bit finicky, it will more than reward your hard work with its immense beauty.

OXALIS TRIANGULARIS

Oxalis

False shamrock

Encompassing more than 500 species, you may be most familiar with the clover-like plants within this far-ranging genus. Their leaves come in a rainbow of colours, from lime green to grey, deep burgundy, blue-green and even gold.

FLOWERS species specific
FAMILY Oxalidaceae
LIGHT filtered/part shade
WATER moderate
SOIL well draining
POSITION indoor/balcony
FROST HARDY no
EXPERT LEVEL novice

Above *Oxalis* leaves sit dainty flowers, most often bell- or tubular-shaped, that tease open as they mature and grow in complementary purples, pinks, yellows, whites and oranges. Most species are nyctinastic, meaning their flowers open when exposed to sun or direct light and close again at night or in cloudy conditions. Their leaves also typically won't open to their full extent in darker conditions.

A special few *Oxalis* species have become very popular house plants. The most common is purple shamrock (*O. triangularis*) with its butterfly-like, deep burgundy leaves that flutter below delicate light purple blooms. Like many *Oxalis*, this plant may enter a period of dormancy and lose its leaves. Ease back on the watering until you see new growth begin to appear.

Some others we adore include the mini tree-like *O. megalorrhiza* and the intoxicatingly geometric *O. palmifrons*. It's worth noting that *Oxalis*, with its ability to thrive, has become weedy (and naturalised) in many regions worldwide. Be conscientious when choosing where to plant it, and opt to grow it in a pot instead of directly in the ground.

FLOWERS spring to summer
FAMILY Papaveraceae
LIGHT full sun
WATER low
SOIL well draining/coarse + sandy
POSITION balcony
FROST HARDY no
EXPERT LEVEL green thumb

ESCHSCHOLZIA CALIFORNICA 'MILKY WAY'

California poppy

The silky soft petals of the state flower of California, *Eschscholzia californica*, sit prettily above the slender grey-green foliage at its base.

Eschscholzia californica

You may be most familiar with the bright orange flowers that blanket meadows or grow along roadsides in its home state, but this sweet species also has many cultivars, including the elegant ruffles of 'Peach sorbet' and buttery lemon goodness of 'Milky way'. The blooms dance with the weather and time of day, closing if the skies go grey or as the sun begins to set.

While it is a productive grower in the wild, it does require a bit of extra attention when domesticated. It will do best in warm climates that don't get too hot in summer. Shield the plant from harsh afternoon rays if the temperature is peaking in midsummer. It does best in nutrient-poor soil, and needs a very well draining potting mix. Be careful not to overwater, as it doesn't fare well in waterlogged soil. It likes a bit of humidity but does require good airflow, so avoid crowding too closely among other plants.

The California poppy is not a cutting flower as the blooms will expire before they make it from pot to vase. Deadhead your plant or allow it to go to seed towards the end of the flowering season to encourage it to self-sow. Keep away from curious creatures as it is toxic.

While *Viola hederacea* makes an incredible ground cover outdoors, it works equally well in containers inside or as part of a balcony garden. Growing along runners that create a mat-like appearance, its spreading growth habit lends it to a spot in a hanging planter, where it can cascade beautifully over the edges of the pot, or as an understorey to a larger potted plant.

This cutie is delightfully undemanding but it does like the soil to be consistently moist, particularly in the warmer months, so it's important to keep on top of watering. A well-draining yet moisture-retaining potting medium will help keep the soil moist but not soggy. Outdoors, it enjoys a filtered or partly shaded spot, and a bright position indoors with some gentle morning sun is also ideal.

It is mainly during the spring and summer that this evergreen perennial will produce its dainty blooms, but given consistently warm temperatures it can flower year round. In addition to enjoying your native violet in situ, its edible blossoms can be used to pretty-up a salad or cake.

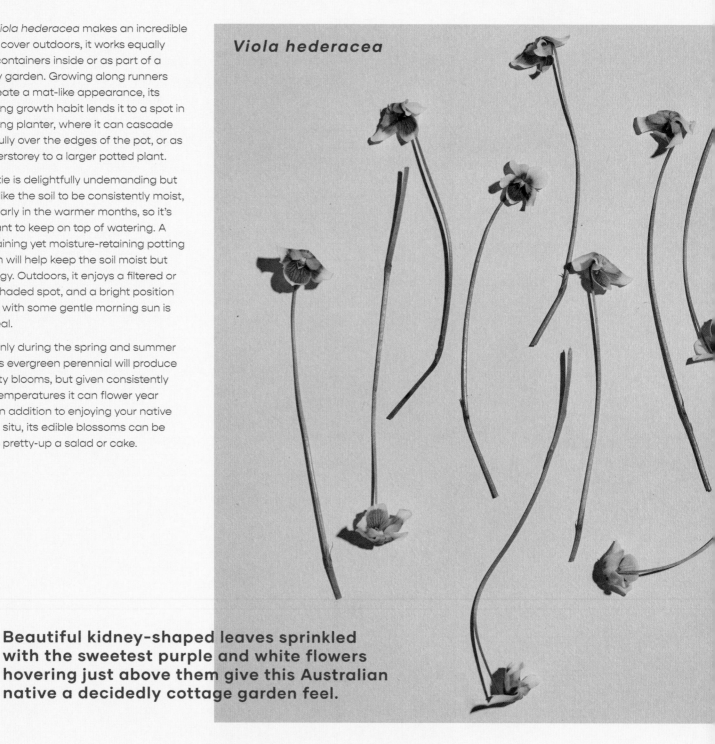

Viola hederacea

Beautiful kidney-shaped leaves sprinkled with the sweetest purple and white flowers hovering just above them give this Australian native a decidedly cottage garden feel.

Native violet

FLOWERS year round
FAMILY Violaceae
LIGHT filtered/part shade
WATER moderate to high
SOIL well draining/
moisture retaining
POSITION indoor/balcony
FROST HARDY no
EXPERT LEVEL novice

FLOWERS mid-spring to summer
FAMILY Ranunculaceae
LIGHT part shade
WATER low to moderate
SOIL well draining/moisture retaining
POSITION balcony
FROST HARDY yes
EXPERT LEVEL
green thumb

AQUILEGIA (SONGBIRD SERIES) 'CARDINAL'

Columbine

Aquilegia hosts around 70 species of perennials most often found growing in nature in dappled sun on the woodland floor. Its delicate foliage, sometimes with bronzed edges, appears far below its sweet flowers.

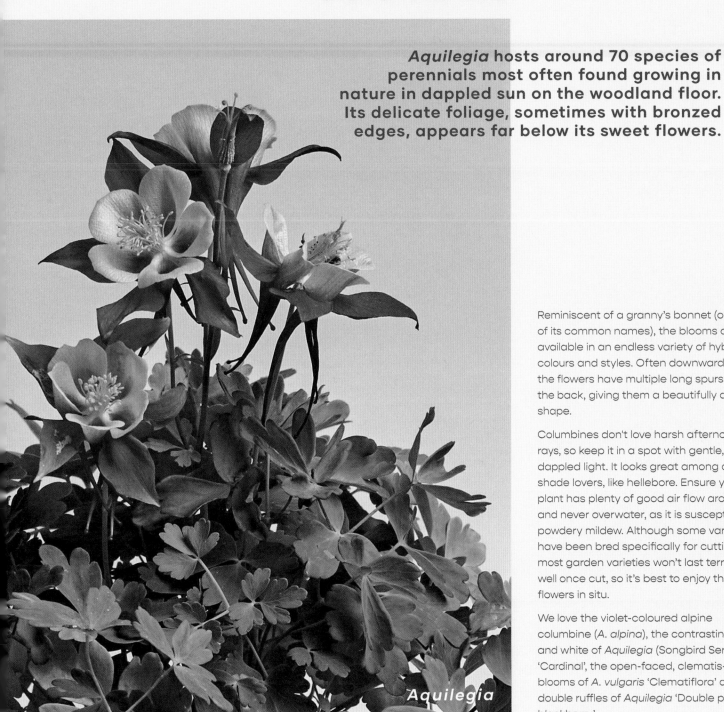

Aquilegia

Reminiscent of a granny's bonnet (one of its common names), the blooms are available in an endless variety of hybridised colours and styles. Often downward facing, the flowers have multiple long spurs at the back, giving them a beautifully distinct shape.

Columbines don't love harsh afternoon rays, so keep it in a spot with gentle, dappled light. It looks great among other shade lovers, like hellebore. Ensure your plant has plenty of good air flow around it and never overwater, as it is susceptible to powdery mildew. Although some varieties have been bred specifically for cutting, most garden varieties won't last terribly well once cut, so it's best to enjoy the flowers in situ.

We love the violet-coloured alpine columbine (*A. alpina*), the contrasting red and white of *Aquilegia* (Songbird Series) 'Cardinal', the open-faced, clematis-like blooms of *A. vulgaris* 'Clematiflora' and the double ruffles of *Aquilegia* 'Double pleat blackberry'.

Delphinium

Although most common in blue, you can also find equally gorgeous *Delphinium* plants with purple, white or rarer red and yellow flowers. The name derives from the Latin word for 'dolphin', reflecting the shape of the spur at the back of the flower.

Delphinium can be quite sensitive to its environment. It generally prefers temperate climates, and does not fare well in storms or too much heat, preferring cooler, wetter summers. If you are in a hotter region, be sure to shield the flowers from overly harsh afternoon sun. In this instance, lots of direct morning sun and dappled afternoon rays are best.

Larger pots are most suited and make sure the plants aren't crowded. Mulch once they become established, to help retain moisture in the potting mix. It takes a lot of energy to produce such showy flowers and the plant will need regular fertilising as soon as a flower spike begins to appear. Slow growth or yellowing foliage can be a sign that the plant is not getting enough nutrients. The hollow stems are brittle so we recommend staking any taller or heavier flower spikes. A tomato cage to provide support around the base will also work well.

Delphinium x *belladonna* is a delicate variety, with light blue, more dispersed flowers. They make a great cut flower but remember that all species are toxic.

With over 250 species of annual and perennial plants, *Delphinium* is best known for its dramatically tall bright blue flower spikes that can grow anywhere from 30 cm to 2 m (12 in to 6½ ft) tall.

Larkspur

FLOWERS spring to summer
FAMILY Ranunculaceae
LIGHT full sun/part shade
WATER moderate to high
SOIL well draining/
moisture retaining
POSITION balcony
FROST HARDY no
EXPERT LEVEL green thumb

The days are long and the sun sits high in the sky. Those plants with the boldest, brightest flowers that can withstand the often harsh, hot conditions of this season will bloom in summer. While some plants will need a little coddling at this time, the strongest will thrive and reward your attentive care with abundance.

summer

Phalaenopsis

Commonly referred to as the moth orchid, due to its wing-like shape, the graceful flower stem of *Phalaenopsis* arches out from a small clump of dark green glossy leaves. The single flower spike is beautiful in its simplicity. Alternatively, for a classic look, mass plant in a large, shallow pot, covering the potting medium with green moss.

This is a tropical orchid that enjoys bright, indirect light and warm, humid conditions. Try standing your pot in a tray of small pebbles filled with water to increase the humidity levels around the plant. Keep it away from air-conditioning units, draughts and excessively hot or cold windows. Feed it with a highly diluted orchid or indoor-specific liquid fertiliser every month or so.

With care, and a bit of luck, it will flower for many years to come. When the flowers fade, cut the stem with a sharp pair of secateurs, 1 cm (½ in) above the lowest node. These as yet 'unused' nodes should be able to produce more blooms in the months ahead. If your plant decides not to push out a second flush and the spike begins to dry out, snip it off at the base and continue to give it lots of care and a very bright position, and another flower spike should appear in 12 months.

From an initial 80 species, thousands of hybrids and cultivars have been produced from the ubiquitous *Phalaenopsis*. There is a good reason for this plant's popularity. As well as being one of the easiest orchids to cultivate, its magnificently showy blooms can last for a very generous three months or more.

Moth orchid

FLOWERS summer
FAMILY Orchidaceae
LIGHT filtered
WATER moderate
SOIL orchid mix
POSITION indoor
FROST HARDY no
EXPERT LEVEL novice

on orchids / Jane Rose Lloyd

A passionate plant lover, Jane Rose Lloyd is a horticulturist, designer and co-owner of Garden Pleasures (formerly The Plant Exchange).

A long-time Leaf Supply collaborator, Jane lent her extensive horticultural knowledge to *Plantopedia* and we're lucky to use her expertise again for *Bloom*. Her greenhouse is filled to the brim with an incredible collection of foliage and flowering specimens.

WHEN DID YOU DISCOVER YOU HAD A SERIOUS AFFINITY WITH PLANTS?

The realisation actually happened twice. The seed was planted when I was very small, maybe three or four years old. Mum was a working single parent so I spent a lot of time with my Oma, which meant spending a lot of time in her garden in Warrandyte (Victoria). For the most part it was an Australian bush garden filled with local indigenous species combined with a few classic interstate natives, mixed in with strong-flowering perennials, roses, citrus and other fruit trees. Oma baked a lot and I have vivid memories of picking flowers and foliage to put around her cakes and in jams. During my rebellious, distracted and unstable teenage years, I lost touch with my connection to plants and with myself. It wasn't until 2016 that I decided to study Applied Horticultural Science in an effort to pull myself out of a bad place and start my own business to support my mental health, and that was it. I was hooked for life.

ABOVE: JANE PICTURED IN HER GREENHOUSE   RIGHT: FINDING THE RIGHT ANGLE ON SOME MEGA *CYMBIDIUM* ORCHIDS

WHAT IS IT ABOUT FLOWERING PLANTS THAT YOU FIND SO CAPTIVATING?

Honestly there are too many things, but if I had to choose just one, it would have to be the sheer diversity seen in flowering plants that really gets me. Not just the various colours and forms they each display in their flowers but ALL the ways in which they differ from one another. We humans are just one species, *Homo sapiens*, but in 2016 a report released by the Royal Botanic Gardens Kew states that of the approximately 391,000 vascular plant species known to science, 369,000 (or 94 per cent) of those are angiosperms or flowering plants. And that's just species we know and have recorded (we describe around 2000 new plant species every year). Imagine how many other species are waiting to be discovered! It's like nature made every single idea it came up with and put them to the test. We are so blessed but, more often than not, blind, not only to plants themselves, but all the crazy, wild, astounding and magical things they can teach us about ourselves.

YOU HAVE AN AMAZING COLLECTION OF ORCHIDS. WHAT IS IT ABOUT THESE PLANTS THAT YOU LOVE SO MUCH?

Orchids have complete control of my heart in the plant world. Orchidaceae is the second-largest plant family, with over 25,000 recorded species (that's twice the number of avian and four times the number of mammalian species), which represents about 10 per cent of all known plants on Earth. Orchids have exploited every climate and environmental niche on the planet, apart from the glaciers, and have the highest concentration of species native to the tropics. If you pay them enough attention – and it doesn't take much – they will capture your soul. You'll fall (truly) both madly and deeply for them and once they've captured your attention, they'll hold it tightly for a lifetime and never let go.

There are so many favourites among this obsession of mine. To pick one is impossible, but *Dendrobium*, *Bulbophyllum* and *Cymbidium* are an excellent place to start looking. However, I would love to highlight our Australian native terrestrial orchids. They are by far one of the most captivating and special groups, and they desperately need our help and attention. Both Sydney's and Melbourne's Royal Botanic Gardens are doing some phenomenal conservation work (you can read about their research on their websites) but conservation always needs the help and attention of the public!

WHEN IT COMES TO CARING FOR FLOWERING PLANTS, AND ORCHIDS IN PARTICULAR, WHAT ARE SOME IMPORTANT FACTORS TO CONSIDER?

Coaxing a plant to flower is often more about luck than it is human input. Plants make their moves based on energy reserves, a complex recipe of environmental factors and, most importantly, timing. For a plant, it's a very precise recipe – it takes weeks, months or even years to collect all the ingredients in perfect measure, to set the temperature just right, to have enough energy in reserves to start the process and still be going all the way through to the finish line AND continue growing after completion. For our best hopes to grow a plant well and to flower it, we need to mimic these processes as best we can. Sometimes this can be seemingly easy – it may be moving a plant to a brighter position or to one with some direct sun, or giving the plant a dry winter rest before daily watering during spring. But sometimes it can be much more complicated, and sometimes it requires years of coaxing and building energy reserves.

The easiest way to make a plant flower is to actively research it, find out its quirks, where it grows and what the environment is like there and do your best to replicate that. Remember, most of the time we'll be growing a plant outside its comfort zone, so we have to 'bridge the environmental gap'. We need to be the summer rain (or monsoon), we need to increase ambient humidity, we need to move the plant so it stays dry and cool during winter. Giving a plant a cup of water every Tuesday and some seaweed solution once a month or so and expecting a nursery-perfect plant with lots of flowers is like eating salt crackers and drinking a jug of water every day or so and expecting to win a 100 m sprint in three weeks. We must work to make the environment add up, and when it does and the timing is right, you'll be amazed by what can grow wonderfully and even bloom for you!

THE WALL OF MOUNTED PLANTS IN YOUR GREENHOUSE IS INTRIGUINGLY BEAUTIFUL. THE FERNS AND ORCHIDS SEEM TO GROW PARTICULARLY WELL THIS WAY. HOW DO YOU MOUNT AND MAINTAIN THEM?

The main reason those plants do so well growing on a mount is because they are epiphytic in nature, meaning they grow rooted to another plant instead of rooted directly in the ground. Their roots are accustomed to copious airflow as they're often growing in the open (like on the side of upright trunks or the undersides of horizontal branches) or only minimally buried in quickly decaying organic matter. Many of them have also evolved to fulfil their moisture and nutrient requirements by absorbing it from the air around them through their roots, so they require a specialised growing environment that can be tricky to maintain at home indoors.

The greenhouse is fully automated and smart, so I can check the temperature and humidity, and control watering, humidity and airflow, from anywhere in the world. Our prime growing parameters are 20–26°C (70–80°F) and 75–90 per cent relative humidity, but I like to harden plants as I grow them so their applications are more versatile for our work, so I open those parameters up to all sorts of extremes like hot, cold, and dry/less humidity.

ABOVE: *DISCHIDIA VIDALII* × SP. 'CAMIGUIN ISLAND'   **RIGHT:** JANE HOLDING HER *DENDROBIUM* 'MEMORIA GARTH GRIFFITH'

How I mount them depends on how they specifically grow in their native environment, mainly pertaining to the amount of moisture-holding and air porosity required to keep their roots happy, which then dictates the exact composition of materials and media I use. I've spent years experimenting with different cultivation methods for mounted plants and it's always a work in progress. I'm still learning and refining my process all the time.

Growing mounted plants successfully can be simplified to adapt to life indoors, but it always comes down to choosing the right plant for the environment. *Platycerium bifurcatum* and *Rhipsalis baccifera* are two excellent easy-care plants to grow on mounts indoors. Give them a lovely bright indirect spot with some morning sun no later than 1 pm, soak them in the shower and hang to drip dry, apply a liquid fertiliser during the growing season and remember they can dry out quickly.

HOW ELSE DO YOU LIKE TO KEEP AND DISPLAY YOUR FLOWERING PLANTS?

I always like to keep my plants as happy as they want, so the majority live in our greenhouse or our nursery area in unattractive nursery pots. I sometimes bring them inside to enjoy their flowering. But mostly I just photograph them endlessly. I've become very selective about who gets to live in the house with us, as they need to be able to tolerate irregular waterings with an occasional brief drought, not be pest magnets and inspire me when I look at them.

A common thread among the plants that live inside with us is their design and architecture. I love sculptural plants, plants with unusual foliage, strange growth habits, huge leaves, plants with impact. In the lounge room I work among many figs, a handful of hardy ferns, some seriously swollen *Sinningia*, and some weirdly winding, bending, twisty things that are totally unrelated to each other.

WHAT ARE SOME OF YOUR OTHER FAVOURITE FLOWERING PLANTS?

Rhipsalis is one of my most favourite genera. They have evolved some fascinating adaptations as members of the cactus family who do not live in deserts but exploit other environmental niches, such as jungle hotspots throughout South America. Anything Araceae that isn't on trend. Anthuriums, philodendrons and similar friends are excellent, don't get me wrong, but I love the freaks and the hard-to-grow, so bulbous aroids such as *Amorphophallus*, *Typhonium*, *Arisaema* to name a few, are some top favourites. *Ficus* is most certainly up there as one of my most favourite genera of all time, as many species are extremely diverse and easygoing, perfect growing for both indoors and outdoors in gardens and on balconies. *Ficus umbellata* and *F. dammaropsis* are currently my top two. Many Australian native plants also hold special spots in my heart, but today's shout-outs go to Acacia, Banksia, Correa and Brachychiton with all their strange freaky species. So much garden goodness to be found in those four alone!

ABOVE: THE HAPPIEST COLLECTION OF PLANTS IN JANE'S INCREDIBLE GREENHOUSE   RIGHT: HIDING BEHIND A STEM OF SPECTACULAR *CYMBIDIUM*

> "The easiest way to make a plant flower is to actively research it, find out its quirks, where it grows and what the environment is like there and do your best to replicate that."

YOU'RE @_STRANGEPLANTLADY ON INSTAGRAM. WHAT ARE SOME OF THE QUIRKIEST FLOWERING PLANTS OUT THERE?

Orchids are definitely in the realm of strange but I shouldn't play favourites. *Ceropegia* species have got to be right up there as some of the strangest plants you're likely to encounter at home (for example, the chain of hearts, *Ceropegia woodii*). Their unusual and seemingly 'ugly' flowers are magnificently designed traps that catch their pollinators in the bottom of an elongated tubular flower that has a narrow waist close to the bottom. Fine hairs inside the flower are delicate enough for insects to easily climb through and down into the flower but, coupled with the cinched waist, make it hard for the insect to make an escape, at least not before rubbing some pollen grains onto the pistils and fertilising the flower. Begonias are definitely among the 'quirkiest' plants. They are so highly adapted to all sorts of weird environmental pockets, they've adopted some of the weirdest appearances of all the plants I can think of. We have a history of not getting along so well but I love *Begonia venosa*, with its papery cataphylls that remind me of cicada wings.

ARE THERE ANY SPOTS IN MELBOURNE OR BEYOND THAT YOU LIKE TO VISIT TO HELP NURTURE YOUR RELATIONSHIP WITH PLANTS?

Botanic gardens are the collective mecca for nurturing relationships with plants! I make a point of visiting Victoria's Royal Botanic Gardens at least once a year to check in and see how much everything has grown since my last visit, and also to take as many photos as I can on a restorative stroll. Botanic gardens deserve more attention and engagement than they receive, as they do exceptional work to further our understanding of plants, their relationship with the world around them and, most importantly, their conservation. I also love visiting 'wilderness' spots like forests and arboretums, national and state parks, even local reserves and linear parks. Anywhere nature is plentiful is always a good place for self-restoration! Some of my most favourite destinations would have to be the Dandenong Ranges, Mount Franklin, Kinglake, Toolangi State Forest and the Black Spur. The south-west botanical province of Western Australia is a bucket-list plant mecca, along with the Gondwana and Daintree rainforests, and South Africa, in particular the Namib Desert to see *Welwitschia mirabilis* (a huge and highly unusual plant) in its natural habitat.

ABOVE AND RIGHT: *DENDROBIUM* 'GOLDEN FLECK'

Erigeron karvinskianus will only grow around 30 cm (12 in) high but will be covered in flowers almost constantly from spring to autumn. Once flowering has finished, cut back to less than 10 cm (4 in) from the base to ensure the plant grows back neat and healthy come the following spring.

As it is considered a weed in some regions (such as parts of Australia and New Zealand), check with your local council before planting in your balcony garden.

FLOWERS spring to autumn
FAMILY Asteraceae
LIGHT full sun/ part shade
WATER moderate
SOIL well draining
POSITION balcony
FROST HARDY yes
EXPERT LEVEL novice

Erigeron karvinskianus

This dainty daisy-like flower is a prolific grower in the right conditions. Often found sprouting from cracks in rock walls or along paths, *Erigeron karvinskianus* also looks great tumbling out of pots.

Seaside daisy

TAGETES PATULA 'BONANZA FLAME' IN A GRETEL CORRIE POT

Marigold

Sunshine in floral form, *Tagetes*, with its bright, happy, warm coloured blooms, is a joyful addition to a balcony garden. Its good looks are attractive not only to humans but also to beneficial insects that can help to deter less-popular ones, like mosquitos.

Tagetes

FLOWERS spring to autumn
FAMILY Asteraceae
LIGHT full sun
WATER moderate
SOIL well draining
POSITION balcony
FROST HARDY no
EXPERT LEVEL novice

Tagetes is perfect for container planting, especially the bushier and more compact French marigolds, but be sure not to crowd them as air circulation is vital for producing healthy plants. Plenty of rays are also key for these sun lovers, who require exposure to at least six hours of sunlight a day.

Care is simple for the easygoing marigold. Be sure to deeply water its well-draining potting mix then allow it to dry out between waterings to avoid root rot and other moisture-related diseases. Watering directly into the potting mix rather than from above will help avoid flower rot. The tips of newly potted plants should be pinched back to encourage thick growth and deadheading flowers will stimulate fresh blooms.

With as many as 2000 species, mainly hailing from tropical and subtropical regions, begonias are incredibly diverse and highly adaptable, thriving indoors and in part shade on a covered balcony.

Their leaves cover a varied spectrum of forms, textures and colour, from the spiral-shaped *Begonia* 'Escargot' to the iridescent and intricately patterned painted-leaf begonias. Their blooms are equally wide-ranging.

While categorising these beautiful plants is a little tricky, there are generally five groups of begonias: rhizomatous, tuberous, cane, wax (also known as semperflorens cultorum group), and rex (or more formally – rex cultorum group). But don't get bogged down in semantics, simply revel in the beauty and diversity of this gorgeous genus of plants.

Begonia

Adored as much for their fabulous foliage as their beautiful blooms, begonias make for the perfect flowering house plant – a double threat if you will.

Begonia

FLOWERS spring to autumn
FAMILY Begoniaceae
LIGHT filtered/part shade
WATER moderate
SOIL well draining
POSITION indoor/balcony
FROST HARDY no
EXPERT LEVEL green thumb

BEGONIA SP.

Rhizomatous begonias (growing from a thick fleshy rhizome along the soil surface) will grow all year round, generally requiring a light prune in spring for general maintenance and to encourage bushy growth. Their clusters of white and pink flowers appear in late winter and into spring.

Growing from tubers, much like potatoes, as their name suggests, tuberous begonias reach a peak of around 50 cm (20 in) in late summer and autumn. They will naturally die back each year, when water should be significantly reduced and yellowing foliage can be cut off.

Featuring cane-like stems, cane begonias (or angel-wing begonias, as they're sometimes called) are wonderfully easy to grow and produce stunningly marked leaves and dainty pendulous clusters of blooms in a variety of colours. A bright position in filtered light indoors and part shade on a balcony will work best, promoting beautiful blooms during spring and summer.

Hybrids originating from B. cucullata, moisture-loving wax begonias thrive in warm, humid conditions. Keeping their rich but well-draining potting mix consistently damp is vital, and they will not take well to the cold so keep temperatures steady too. They grow well indoors in a very bright position and can tolerate direct morning sun.

For those with a penchant for foliage, rex begonias are the ticket. Hybrids descended from the Indian species B. rex, they produce small, unshowy blooms but they have strikingly beautiful leaves. Growers of rex begonias (commonly known as painted lady begonias) often pinch off blooms so the plants can focus their energy on strong foliage growth.

FLOWERS spring to summer
FAMILY Lamiaceae
LIGHT full sun
WATER low
SOIL coarse + sandy
POSITION indoor
FROST HARDY
species dependent
EXPERT LEVEL novice

LAVANDULA STOECHAS

Lavender

A treat for the olfactory system as well as the eyes, the beautifully soothing scent of lavender along with its softly stunning flowers make *Lavandula* an essential plant for bringing some much-needed calm to your garden.

Lavandula

Growing largely throughout the mountainous regions of the Mediterranean, it is also native to India and Northern Africa. This ubiquitous herb comes in many varieties, offering a vast selection of bloom times, colours, flower forms and sizes.

Contrary to popular thought, not all lavenders are purple. Some hybrids come in other lovely pastel hues such as blue, pink, white and even yellow. The leaves can also vary in shape and colour. To extend the bloom season as well as the colour palette, consider planting several varieties.

Indoors, your *Lavandula* plants will need at least four hours of direct sunlight, so pop them near a window. Outdoors, they will also lap up the sun. They enjoy a breeze, so open a window and don't crowd them among other plants. Use a clay or terracotta pot filled with a well-draining potting mix. Lavender will thrive in poor, dry soil, so don't overwater and use only a little half-strength fertiliser once or twice a year. Your plant, indoor or out, will need pruning after the first flowering, and then again before growth slows for the winter.

French lavender, which has a softer scent and the longest-flowering blooms, is the easiest to grow indoors. Sprigs of its foliage or flowers can be used to garnish salads and flavour desserts and drinks. Or do as the Romans did, and add a stem or two to your bath.

FLOWERS late spring
to early autumn
FAMILY Dioscoreaceae
LIGHT filtered/part shade
WATER moderate to high
SOIL well draining
POSITION indoor/balcony
FROST HARDY no
EXPERT LEVEL green thumb

TACCA INTEGRIFOLIA

White batflower

If you're in any doubt about the magic of Mother Nature, *Tacca integrifolia* with its awe-inspiring and intricate whiskered blooms will set you straight. Grown mainly for its flowers, its large, ribbed foliage is lovely in its own right, making this an excellent year-round addition to an indoor or balcony garden for those lucky enough to get their hands on this rare beauty.

Native to the tropical and subtropical rainforests of Central Asia, *T. integrifolia* is a herb and member of the yam family. Commonly referred to as the white batflower for the form of its incredible blooms that are reminiscent of a bat in full flight, there is an equally special black species (*T. chantrieri*) that is more petite and slightly harder to cultivate.

When *T. integrifolia* has reached maturity – generally once it has produced a pair of full-sized leaves – given the right care, it should start producing blooms from late spring through to early autumn and can do so up to eight times in one growing season. Talk about prolific! The best care involves high levels of humidity, a very well draining potting medium and access to excellent airflow (similar to orchid care).

Consistent watering that keeps the potting mix moist but never soggy is important. Potted plants will enjoy being watered by submerging the whole pot into a bucket of water until air bubbles stop and then allowing excess water to drain off. The trick is to get the right balance, so that the plant is sufficiently moist but the roots aren't sitting in stagnant water and causing rot.

Outdoors, they will do best in a shaded position that mimics their natural habitat – on the rainforest floor, shaded by the canopy above. A bright position indoors away from any direct sun is also suitable, but if the plant struggles to flower it might be best to move it outside. Thankfully, they experience few issues with pests but on a balcony you will need to keep an eye out for snails and slugs that will happily feast on their lush foliage.

ROSMARINUS OFFICINALIS 'PROSTRATUS' IN A LEAF AND THREAD PLANTER

Rosmarinus officinalis

Rosemary

An evergreen shrub that really needs little introduction, *Rosmarinus officinalis* produces beautiful clusters of pale blue flowers in addition to its needle-like foliage that is an essential culinary herb.

FLOWERS late spring to summer
FAMILY Lamiaceae
LIGHT full sun/direct
WATER moderate
SOIL well draining
POSITION indoor/balcony
FROST HARDY yes
EXPERT LEVEL novice

Bringing an intoxicatingly intense aroma and attracting a plethora of pollinators, *Rosmarinus* is an excellent addition to a balcony garden that receives plenty of sun.

While rosemary can survive indoors, many people make the mistake of bringing it inside without any acclimatisation and the sudden reduction in direct sun can have devastating effects. It is advisable to reduce the amount of sun the plant gets over a period of a few weeks. Once inside, be sure to position it in a bright spot, preferably on a windowsill where it will receive six hours of direct sun. Indoors or out, once established it is wonderfully drought tolerant and will do best in a well-draining potting medium, even growing well in a sandy, less fertile mix. A hardy and versatile beauty indeed.

R. officinalis 'Prostratus', or creeping rosemary, is a lovely plant with a creeping habit that makes it less susceptible to wind damage in an exposed position.

Salvia farinacea is in the same family as rosemary, sage and lavender, so you'll notice the obvious visual similarities in their blooms and popularity with pollinators. We love watching the bees hover around our salvias, taking pleasure in the little landing zone the plants have cleverly grown as part of their flower – a comfy spot for pollinators to rest while they nuzzle around for pollen.

Moderately drought tolerant once established, *S. farinacea* will still need to be watered regularly when planted in pots, which will inevitably dry out more readily than a garden bed. These plants do require lots of sun to grow to full height and produce happy blooms. Too little sun and they'll be prone to fungal problems.

S. farinacea is one of the more compact salvias, growing roughly 60 cm (2 ft) tall, and will benefit from a serious prune after flowering to allow it to direct energy into healthy fresh growth in spring. In a container, this perennial will probably only last five years. Try one of its many cultivars when you're ready for a refresh.

Salvia farinacea

Of all the salvias (and there a lot of species and cultivars out there), *Salvia farinacea* is one of our favourites. Its deep violet-blue flower spikes pop against its bright green leaves and provide a lovely bit of height in a garden.

Mealy sage

FLOWERS spring to autumn
FAMILY Lamiaceae
LIGHT full sun
WATER moderate
SOIL well draining
POSITION balcony
FROST HARDY only just
EXPERT LEVEL novice

FLOWERS late spring until autumn/frost
FAMILY Lythraceae
LIGHT full sun
WATER moderate
SOIL well draining
POSITION balcony
FROST HARDY no
EXPERT LEVEL novice

CUPHEA x PURPUREA (CUPHEA 'HONEYBELLS')

Mouse flower

Producing foliage and flowers in a diverse range of colours, shapes and sizes, *Cuphea* is an easygoing annual with an extended blooming period.

Cuphea

With a generally compact and bushy growth habit, *Cuphea* is ideal for container planting, mixing beautifully with a variety of other plants.

While the blooms are generally petite and tubular in appearance, what they lack in stature they more than make up for in quantity, and they are wonderful for attracting pollinators. In a vast array of shades from orange through to neon pink and a multitude of combinations, many varieties feature flowers with modified petals that resemble oversized ears, which inspired its common name.

Most varieties of *Cuphea* require an abundance of direct sun to ensure the greatest flush of blooms and avoid etiolated growth. During the growing season, ensure the well-draining potting mix is kept consistently moist, although established plants are more drought tolerant. To keep plants looking their best, occasional pruning will be appreciated.

CEROPEGIA AMPLIATA

Ceropegia ampliata

Bushman's pipe

Fleshy stems covered in striking, bulbous, flask-shaped flowers make for a quirky plant indeed and its common names – bushman's pipe, condom plant and horny wonder – only add to the intrigue.

FLOWERS late summer to autumn
FAMILY Apocynaceae
LIGHT direct/part shade to full sun
WATER low
SOIL coarse + sandy
POSITION indoor/balcony
FROST HARDY no
EXPERT LEVEL novice

Ceropegia ampliata is native to South Africa, where it grows in scrub and on rocky hillsides, twining among other vegetation. Coming from this hot, dry environment means it is exceedingly drought tolerant, doesn't tolerate temperatures below about 16°C (60°F) and requires a sandy and coarse potting mix to keep its roots from becoming waterlogged.

With immature and insignificant deciduous leaves, it is the blooms that are the real star of the show – by late summer, the white and green flowers will hopefully appear in abundance. Interestingly, it is generally flies that pollinate *Ceropegia*, with the tubular structure of the flowers specifically adapted to capture them. Insects become trapped inside the flower thanks to a lining of hairs that force them down to where the pollen is housed. Only when the flower has wilted can the pollinators escape with the pollen attached to their bodies, ready to be transferred to another plant.

As a house plant, bushman's pipe will do best in a very bright position with access to around four hours of direct sun each day. While it will live happily indoors, once it is flowering, it is best to relocate it to an outdoor position. A monthly feed with liquid fertiliser in the active growing period is more than sufficient, but feeding should be reduced in winter, and watering must also be significantly reduced.

Hoyas produce blooms in combinations of pink, yellow, green, red, peach, white and near black. The most common are *Hoya carnosa*, with soft pink blooms, and *H. pubicalyx*, with green and silver variegated foliage. The flowers of some species are velutinous, others have more pointed petals, and many are sweetly scented. Many hoya species will bloom sporadically throughout the year, generally hitting their peak in summer.

This is a plant that thrives indoors. While a handful of species will happily bloom in indirect light or shade, many need a bit more sun in order to bloom. Watering is also a key factor, with most species requiring their potting mix to stay relatively dry. Some species will also require cooler temperatures (and reduced watering) over winter to bloom.

Hoyas love being a little rootbound, so don't rush to repot. They aren't heavy feeders – a small dose of well-diluted fertiliser during the flowering periods should suffice. Hoyas prefer not to be pruned, and you don't want to accidentally chop off the point from which new flowers will appear. Simply allow their stems to trail over a well-weighted pot or encourage them to climb up a trellis or hooks on a wall.

Once you start diving into the world of hoyas, it's easy to understand why people become obsessed with collecting them.

Hoya

Hoyas are special plants. Their foliage is as delightful as their beautiful blooms, and that says a lot, as their umbels of sweet starburst flowers are certainly outstanding.

Wax plant

FAMILY spring to summer,
sometimes year round
FAMILY Apocynaceae
LIGHT filtered/part shade
WATER low to moderate
SOIL well draining
POSITION indoor/balcony
FROST HARDY no
EXPERT LEVEL novice

HOSTA PLANTAGINEA 'GRANDIFLORA' IN A PLANTER HANDMADE BY RICH CAMILLERI

Hosta

Plantain lily

Hosta is generally grown for its lush, ribbed foliage rather than its flowers, but there are a few species with particularly pretty blooms. Our favourites are *Hosta* 'Blue mouse ears' with its blue-green leaves and light purple flowers, and *H. plantaginea* 'Grandiflora' with its bright apple green leaves and strongly perfumed white flowers, reminiscent of the scent of tuberose and gardenia.

FLOWERS summer to autumn
FAMILY Asparagaceae
LIGHT filtered/full shade/part shade
WATER moderate
SOIL well draining
POSITION indoor/balcony
FROST HARDY yes
EXPERT LEVEL novice

A clumping, herbaceous perennial native to Japan, there are over 2500 cultivars from an original 40 or so different species. The leaves vary in colour from light to dark green, blues, greys and variegations in yellow and white. The flowers, some showier than others, sit high above the leaf line.

This shade-loving, low-maintenance plant does well indoors and outside. A spot with a bit of gentle but direct morning sun will help growth and the continuation of any desired variegations. While young, it will need its potting mix kept moist, but once it has matured it will be a bit more tolerant of drier conditions. *Hosta* can be prone to snails and slugs, so keep a beer trap nearby. Don't be alarmed when the foliage dies back in winter, as it will return in force come spring. *Hosta* can be easily divided by slicing the plant in half, roots and all, and makes a great gift.

FLOWERS late spring
to early summer
FAMILY Apocynaceae
LIGHT full sun
WATER moderate
SOIL well draining
POSITION balcony
FROST HARDY no
EXPERT LEVEL novice

MANDEVILLA 'ALOHA BRIGHT WHITE'

Rocktrumpet

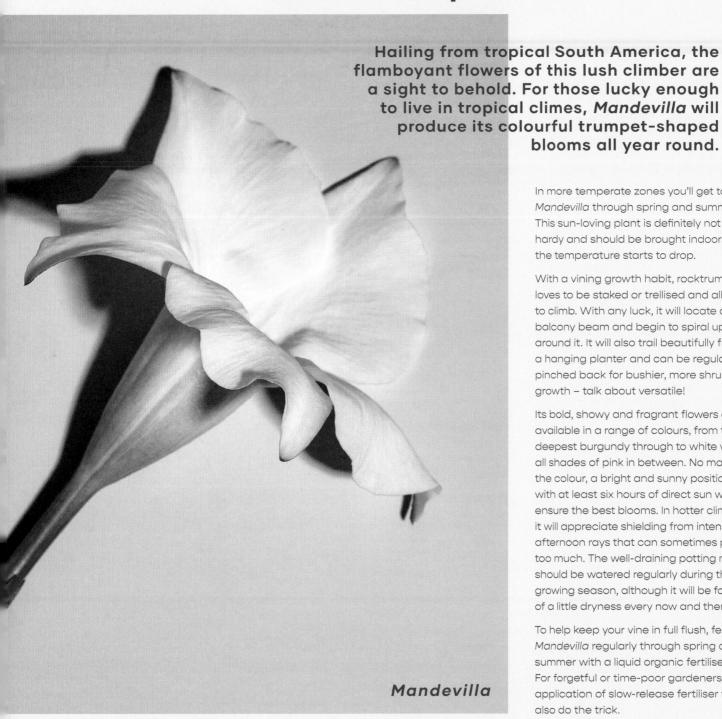

Hailing from tropical South America, the flamboyant flowers of this lush climber are a sight to behold. For those lucky enough to live in tropical climes, *Mandevilla* will produce its colourful trumpet-shaped blooms all year round.

In more temperate zones you'll get to enjoy *Mandevilla* through spring and summer. This sun-loving plant is definitely not frost hardy and should be brought indoors once the temperature starts to drop.

With a vining growth habit, rocktrumpet loves to be staked or trellised and allowed to climb. With any luck, it will locate a balcony beam and begin to spiral up and around it. It will also trail beautifully from a hanging planter and can be regularly pinched back for bushier, more shrub-like growth – talk about versatile!

Its bold, showy and fragrant flowers are available in a range of colours, from the deepest burgundy through to white with all shades of pink in between. No matter the colour, a bright and sunny position with at least six hours of direct sun will ensure the best blooms. In hotter climates, it will appreciate shielding from intense afternoon rays that can sometimes prove too much. The well-draining potting mix should be watered regularly during the growing season, although it will be forgiving of a little dryness every now and then.

To help keep your vine in full flush, feed *Mandevilla* regularly through spring and summer with a liquid organic fertiliser. For forgetful or time-poor gardeners, an application of slow-release fertiliser will also do the trick.

Mandevilla

Ceropegia linearis subsp. *woodii* (also known as *Ceropegia woodii*) trails beautifully, so a hanging planter or shelf position is ideal for displaying its cascading stems. A very bright position indoors where it receives plenty of filtered light will keep the chain of hearts looking its best and help promote blooms. It will also live happily on a covered balcony, sheltered from the elements and harsher afternoon rays, where its delicate flowers can attract pollinators, generally small flies and – if you live somewhere lucky enough to have them – hummingbirds.

In addition to its good looks, chain of hearts is delightfully easy to care for, with overwatering being the main culprit for any issues that might arise. Its semi-succulent leaves mean its water needs are relatively low, so ensure the very well draining potting mix is allowed to dry out between drinks.

For added charm, opt for *C. woodii* f. *variegata*, whose foliage is beautifully mottled with cream, pink and green.

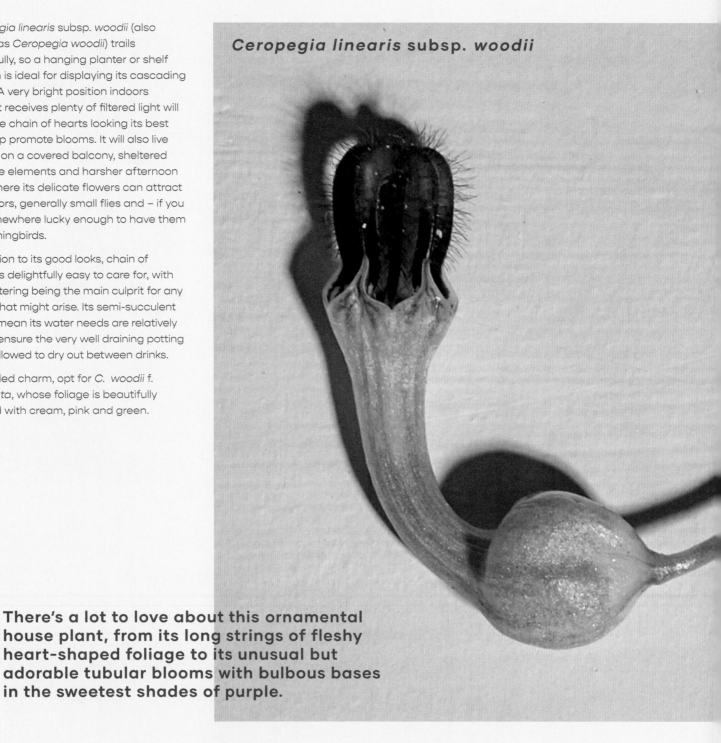

Ceropegia linearis subsp. *woodii*

There's a lot to love about this ornamental house plant, from its long strings of fleshy heart-shaped foliage to its unusual but adorable tubular blooms with bulbous bases in the sweetest shades of purple.

Chain of hearts

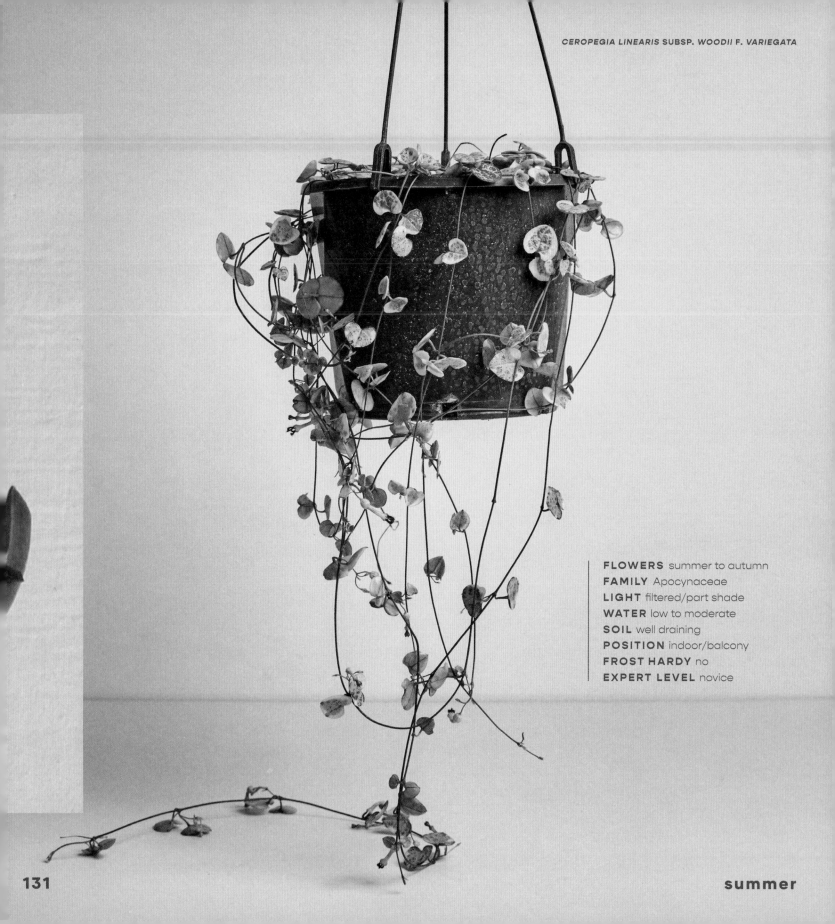

FLOWERS summer to autumn
FAMILY Apocynaceae
LIGHT filtered/part shade
WATER low to moderate
SOIL well draining
POSITION indoor/balcony
FROST HARDY no
EXPERT LEVEL novice

ARISTOLOCHIA GRANDIFLORA

Aristolochia

Pelican flower

The genus *Aristolochia* contains over 400 species of tropical plants with incredibly arresting flowers. Most often vining, they are prized for their unusual looks that reflect some of their common names – birthwort (resembling a birth canal), Dutchman's pipe, pipevine and pelican flower.

FLOWERS spring to autumn
FAMILY Aristolochiaceae
LIGHT filtered
WATER moderate to high
SOIL well draining/
moisture retaining
POSITION indoor/balcony
FROST HARDY no
EXPERT LEVEL
green thumb

The pelican flower (*A. grandiflora*), one of the largest flowers in the world, took our breath away when we first stumbled across it at the University of Basel Botanical Garden. With flowers that grow up to 20 cm (8 in) wide and 60 cm (2 ft) long, it appears heart-shaped from the front and bulbous from the side, with a very long tail trailing below. Cream in colour, and covered in burgundy veins, the centre of the heart opens into a dark cave that emits a rotten smell. This scent attracts pollinators, mainly flies, who enter and become trapped in the back chamber (where the reproductive organs reside) by the fine hairs covering the inside of the flower. It is only when the plant registers that an adequate amount of pollen has been released onto the bug that it relaxes the hairs and allows the pollinator to escape. This whole process often takes two days – quite the ordeal for both plant and pollinator. Other species, such as *A. arborea*, whose blooms appear from mid-trunk, look and even smell like particular mushrooms to attract a very specific pollinator: the mushroom gnat.

Some varieties are considered noxious weeds in certain regions (such as Australia), so always double-check before planting them in your garden. Keep them in pots and ensure any fruit or seeds are carefully disposed of before they have a chance to mature. The plants are highly toxic so it is best not to grow them if you have curious pets or children around. When handling the plant, always wear gloves.

Portulaca grandiflora's chubby leaves, which retain loads of water and make it drought tolerant, are complemented by little flowers measuring around 3 cm (1 in) in diameter that come in a variety of pinks, yellows, reds, oranges, purples, creams and whites. It is a delightful double-flowering plant that reminds us of miniature tree peonies.

Super low maintenance, this plant loves the heat and is often found growing in cracks of rocks or out of old buildings – similar to the seaside daisy (*Erigeron karvinskianus*). Don't overwater, steer clear of over-fertilising, and you'll find that it will flourish with a distinct lack of attention. Keep an eye on it to ensure that it doesn't take over, and deadhead most of the flowers so they don't self-sow everywhere.

Like its cousin, the potentially better known and edible purslane (*P. oleracea*), it is considered a weed in some areas, so plant thoughtfully.

Portulaca grandiflora

Hailing from Brazil, this fun and easygoing succulent is a hardy annual that should self-sow and come back year after year.

Moss rose

FLOWERS summer
FAMILY Portulacaceae
LIGHT full sun
WATER low
SOIL well draining/
coarse + sandy
POSITION balcony
FROST HARDY no
EXPERT LEVEL novice

FLOWERS summer
to early autumn
FAMILY Asteraceae
LIGHT full sun
WATER low to moderate
SOIL well draining/
coarse + sandy
POSITION balcony
FROST HARDY yes
EXPERT LEVEL novice

Golden marguerite

Commonly known as golden marguerite (*marguerite* means 'daisy' in French), this daisy-like flower has yellow-cream blooms that sit high above faintly aromatic feathery foliage, and will flower all through summer and even into early autumn if you provide it with the right care.

Cota tinctoria (syn. *Anthemis tinctoria*) is from the same family as chamomile, and its tall flowers, great for cutting, are adored by butterflies and bees.

Not a fan of tropical conditions, it prefers more temperate climes. As in nature, it appreciates well-draining and slightly sandy soil and does not require much in the way of fertiliser. A small addition of nutrients once a year during the growing season should suffice.

Although it can be relatively drought tolerant once established, a low to moderate watering schedule will ensure bountiful flowers in summer. Continue to deadhead throughout the flowering season to ensure flush after flush of blooms. When the season has eventually ended, give your plant a ruthless prune to keep it looking neat and tidy.

Cota tinctoria

Striking and sculptural, the dahlia is a classic cutting flower. Available in an incredible variety of colours and forms, its size is widely variable, ranging from the largest dinner-plate dahlias to dwarf varieties that work beautifully in containers.

Dahlia
Dahlia

FLOWERS late summer to autumn
FAMILY Asteraceae
LIGHT full sun/part shade
WATER moderate
SOIL well draining
POSITION balcony
FROST HARDY no
EXPERT LEVEL novice

Along with its impressive good looks, *Dahlia* is relatively easy to grow and looks equally beautiful in situ or as part of a cut floral display.

Given the diversity of dahlias available, it's best to base your choice not only on the type of bloom you're after but also on their environmental suitability and the plant's eventual size. *Dahlia* 'Mystic haze' is a bushy, clump-forming variety with orange-yellow blooms that pop from its deep purple foliage. This relatively petite plant makes an excellent home on a small balcony.

Dinner-plate dahlias, as they are affectionately known, such as *Dahlia* 'Cafe au lait', will need much more room to grow and will generally require staking of its tall, heavy blooms. Other varieties we love include *Dahlia* 'Henriette' with its salmon pink flowers and spiky petals (placing it in the semi-cactus category of dahlias, with double flowers, star-like shape and folded, spiky-looking petals), and *Dahlia* 'Gitty up', with its fluffy red centres and flat outer petals (an anemone dahlia, with outer petals framing a dramatic pincushion of disc florets in the centre).

Dahlia tubers are best planted in spring about 10 cm (4 in) deep. Too much water in the early stages can cause the tuber to rot, so they should be kept only lightly watered until the plant is established and reaches about 15 cm (6 in). A full-sun to part-shade position sheltered from strong winds will work best. Dahlias are known as tender perennials, meaning they can live for many years but will need to be brought inside for overwintering in cooler climates.

ALOCASIA BAGINDA 'SILVER DRAGON'

Alocasia baginda 'Silver dragon'
Alocasia silver dragon

Many indoor plants are kept for their fabulous foliage alone and sporting some particularly incredible leaves, *Alocasia baginda* 'Silver dragon' is one such species.

FLOWERS late spring
to summer
FAMILY Araceae
LIGHT filtered
WATER moderate to high
SOIL well draining
POSITION indoor
FROST HARDY no
EXPERT LEVEL expert

While its flowers are often considered secondary and are simply removed to allow the plant to focus its energy on leaf growth, they are certainly worth a mention.

It is important to note right off the bat that this is not a plant for the novice gardener. Classified as a 'jewel' *Alocasia* for its beauty and petite stature, this plant is incredibly demanding in the care stakes. It is rare for it to flower indoors and it is only under very specific conditions that you are likely to see any blooms at all.

A cultivar of *A. baginda*, a Borneo native, 'Silver dragon' features ghostly silvery green leaves with a dark centre and a luminous tone. The incredible texture, strong contrast and dark venation ensure the leaf's resemblance to a dragon's scale and the inspiration for its common name.

Far from showy, the blooms of this *Alocasia* are not dissimilar from those of the peace lily or flamingo flower, consisting of a white or green spoon-like shell surrounding the spadix. They tend to appear during late spring and into summer and last for a brief few days.

For expert gardeners who are lucky enough to achieve blooms, it is possible to pollinate the flowers manually to produce seeds or hybrid plants. The male and female parts of the inflorescence are separate and are fertile at different times to prevent self-fertilisation. To facilitate pollination, the pollen must be collected and stored until the female flowers are ripe. Then it can be transferred using a small artist's brush. Certainly a worthy challenge for the seasoned collector.

Eomecon chionantha

Eomecon chionantha, commonly known as snow poppy (and sometimes dawn poppy or Chinese bloodroot), has large grey-green leaves with scalloped edges, and tall delicate flowers. Four pure white petals surround a golden mass of stamens, peeking high above the leaf line. Its flowers remind us of dogwood in their colour and symmetry.

While *E. chionantha* won't reach higher than 50 cm (20 in), it can spread rapidly in nutrient rich soil, reaching up to 4 m (13 ft) wide, so it's best to keep it contained in a pot, as it may be invasive in some areas. It enjoys direct morning rays and some afternoon sun too, as long as the soil is kept moist all year round.

Flowers appear in spring, and depending on the climate, may last until the midsummer. Come autumn, seeds can be collected once they have dried on the plant, and when winter rolls around the plant remains relatively frost hardy.

Native to the moist riverbanks and forests of eastern China, this rhizomatous perennial is a new favourite of ours.

Snow poppy

FLOWERS late spring to summer
FAMILY Papaveraceae
LIGHT part shade
WATER moderate to high
SOIL moisture retaining/
well draining
POSITION balcony
FROST HARDY yes
EXPERT LEVEL novice

FLOWERS summer to autumn
FAMILY Asteraceae
LIGHT full sun
WATER low to moderate
SOIL well draining
POSITION balcony
FROST HARDY yes
EXPERT LEVEL novice

RUDBECKIA SP.

Coneflower

The brightly coloured petals of *Rudbeckia* surround a dramatically dark central cone, from which its common names, black-eyed susan and coneflower, are derived.

Rudbeckia

A member of the Asteraceae family, *Rudbeckia* produces daisy-like flowers, most commonly blooming in the happiest of bright yellows. There is a variety of species and cultivars in a range of sunset hues – oranges and reds or dramatic combinations of the two. It looks right at home in a cottage garden–style balcony, and their hairy stems are long and strong, making them a great cutting flower.

Rudbeckia is a very low maintenance plant that will reward what little care you give them with flowers for months over summer. It loves lots of direct rays, and blooms that grow well and straight towards the sun are a good indication that its needs are being sufficiently met.

A fortnightly feed with liquid fertiliser during the flowering period can improve the size and number of blooms. Keeping the soil moist and deadheading flowers as they begin to fade will also help. Delightfully, coneflowers attract a plethora of pollinators, bringing even more life and joy to the garden.

Gone are the days of hydrangeas being relegated to Nanna's garden. The huge, fluffy blooms are well and truly back in vogue and we're here for it.

Hydrangea
Hortensia

FLOWERS summer to autumn
FAMILY Hydrangeaceae
LIGHT part shade/full sun
WATER moderate
SOIL well draining
POSITION balcony
FROST HARDY no
EXPERT LEVEL novice

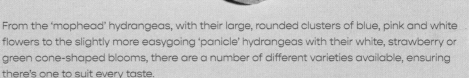
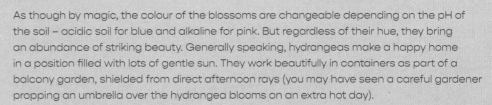

From the 'mophead' hydrangeas, with their large, rounded clusters of blue, pink and white flowers to the slightly more easygoing 'panicle' hydrangeas with their white, strawberry or green cone-shaped blooms, there are a number of different varieties available, ensuring there's one to suit every taste.

As though by magic, the colour of the blossoms are changeable depending on the pH of the soil – acidic soil for blue and alkaline for pink. But regardless of their hue, they bring an abundance of striking beauty. Generally speaking, hydrangeas make a happy home in a position filled with lots of gentle sun. They work beautifully in containers as part of a balcony garden, shielded from direct afternoon rays (you may have seen a careful gardener propping an umbrella over the hydrangea blooms on an extra hot day).

Described as a 'gross feeder', hydrangeas are hungry beasts that will appreciate a regular feed through spring and summer and a rich potting mix with plenty of organic matter. While they lie dormant through winter, they burst back to life come spring. Adding some slow-release fertiliser when planting can help get them on their way.

New flowers will form on the growth from the previous year, so pruning plays a vital role in hydrangea maintenance. Give them a heavy trim in winter, removing dead wood and unproductive shoots. Once in bloom, do away with spent flowers, trimming just 2–5 cm (¾–2 in) above a pair of buds, and you'll be rewarded with a further flush of flowers.

STREPTOCARPUS CAULESCENS

Nodding violet

Sporting sumptuous velvety foliage in the lushest of greens with the sweetest violet trumpet-shaped blooms suspended above on delicate curved stems, *Streptocarpus caulescens* is a popular house plant for good reason.

FLOWERS year round in some conditions, peaking in summer
FAMILY Gesneriaceae
LIGHT filtered/part shade
WATER moderate
SOIL well draining
POSITION indoor/balcony
FROST HARDY no
EXPERT LEVEL novice

Streptocarpus caulescens

This easy-care beauty looks fabulous in a hanging planter where its sleepy blooms can be admired from below. While its growth tends to get a little leggy in the warmer months, regular trims will help to keep the plant more compact and full.

FLOWERS spring to autumn
FAMILY Rosaceae
LIGHT full sun
WATER moderate
SOIL well draining,
ideally rose-specific
POSITION balcony
FROST HARDY yes
EXPERT LEVEL green thumb

ROSA NOASCHNEE 'RED' IN A TERRACOTTA HAYLEY WEST PLANTER

Rose

The classic rose has captured the imagination of humans for millennia. Making use of around 150 species, thousands upon thousands of cultivars have been created. From simple, single-petal varieties to large, blousy blooms, in all manner of heavenly scents, and in almost every colour you can imagine, roses are grown in gardens all over the world as well as in huge numbers for the floristry and perfume industries.

This woody perennial generally enjoys temperate and cool conditions. It requires upwards of six hours of direct sunlight each day, so find a sunny spot on your balcony, away from any thoroughfare so the thorns won't scratch passers-by. The pot should be fairly well protected from harsh rays, as the roots don't appreciate overheating. Smaller varieties, such as *Rosa noaschnee* 'Red', will better suit container gardens.

All roses require a fertile potting mix and it's best to use a rose-specific one. Top the nutrients up in spring, giving regular doses while your plant is in bloom and add a layer of mulch as the weather warms. Water your rose directly into the potting mix, avoiding wetting the flowers and leaves, which can be prone to mildew or rot.

Deadhead your rose once its blooms are spent and remove any dead branches. Most rose species are deciduous, so expect them to go bare over winter. Prune in late winter to early spring. Treat it to a really solid cut back – approximately one-half to two-thirds of the plant. Use sharp secateurs, cut just above leaf nodes and also remove the central stems on more compact plants.

Rosa

From the incredibly textured ripple varieties with deeply ridged round foliage to the dainty, emerald green leaves of *Peperomia* 'Amigo Marcello', these generally petite but pretty plants are a popular indoor choice for good reason.

In contrast, its flowers are decidedly unshowy. In the summer months, *Peperomia* produces long, slim flower spikes that, in most cases, take a back seat to their striking foliage. It is not uncommon for people to pinch off blooms to allow the plant to focus energy on producing fresh leaves.

If you are a fan of the unique blooms, you will need to provide plenty of bright, filtered light, avoiding direct afternoon sun that will damage that special foliage. Once the flowers are spent, remove them from the plant, cutting with sharp secateurs as close to the base as possible.

Many *Peperomia* varieties grow epiphytically, so an orchid potting mix is perfect for providing the drainage they need. Keep the medium relatively moist but never soggy. Even the most novice of gardeners will rejoice, as this is a hardy plant that will tolerate some neglect with aplomb.

Peperomia

Generally grown and adored for its glorious leaves, *Peperomia* is fabulously varied, for the most part featuring fleshy, almost succulent, leaves.

Radiator plant

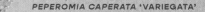

PEPEROMIA CAPERATA 'VARIEGATA'

FLOWERS summer
FAMILY Piperaceae
LIGHT filtered
WATER moderate
SOIL well draining/
orchid mix
POSITION indoor
FROST HARDY no
EXPERT LEVEL novice

153   **summer**

FLOWERS summer to autumn
FAMILY Onagraceae
LIGHT full sun
WATER low to moderate
SOIL well draining/
coarse + sandy
POSITION balcony
FROST HARDY no
EXPERT LEVEL novice

OENOTHERA LINDHEIMERI 'LILLIPOP SODA POP'

Bee blossoms

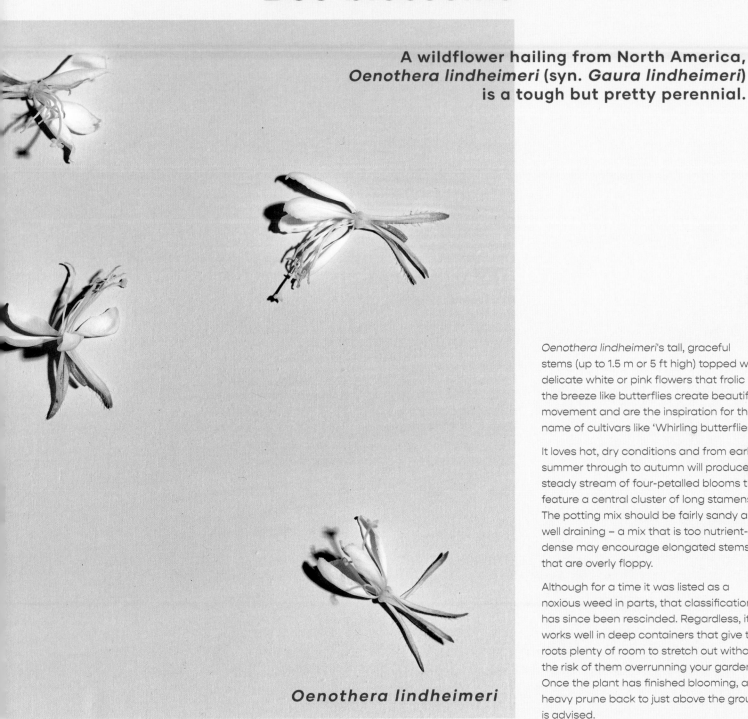

A wildflower hailing from North America, *Oenothera lindheimeri* (syn. *Gaura lindheimeri*) is a tough but pretty perennial.

Oenothera lindheimeri

Oenothera lindheimeri's tall, graceful stems (up to 1.5 m or 5 ft high) topped with delicate white or pink flowers that frolic in the breeze like butterflies create beautiful movement and are the inspiration for the name of cultivars like 'Whirling butterflies'.

It loves hot, dry conditions and from early summer through to autumn will produce a steady stream of four-petalled blooms that feature a central cluster of long stamens. The potting mix should be fairly sandy and well draining – a mix that is too nutrient-dense may encourage elongated stems that are overly floppy.

Although for a time it was listed as a noxious weed in parts, that classification has since been rescinded. Regardless, it works well in deep containers that give the roots plenty of room to stretch out without the risk of them overrunning your garden. Once the plant has finished blooming, a heavy prune back to just above the ground is advised.

Pelargonium is a regular contender at flower shows and has even been claimed as the national flower of Switzerland. When you add in the fact that they're easy to care for and have long-lasting flowers, how could you say no to this bold and beautiful plant?

Originally thought to be part of the *Geranium* genus, genetic tests have now moved many plants into this newer genus, most easily differentiated by its flowers. While *Geranium* species have five petals all symmetrically appearing from a central point, *Pelargonium* species have two top and three lower petals.

Pelargonium

When you think of *Pelargonium* – one of the most popular decorative plants of all time – your mind might take you to a Spanish home with walls covered in terracotta pots bursting with red blooms, or hanging planters framing alpine towns with cascading flowers in a rainbow of colours.

Geranium

FLOWERS summer to autumn
FAMILY Geraniaceae
LIGHT part shade/full sun
WATER low to moderate
SOIL well draining
POSITION balcony
FROST HARDY
species dependent
EXPERT LEVEL novice

In the *Pelargonium* genus, you will find a huge diversity of plants, from the large showy floral clusters of the regal varieties to the beautifully perfumed leaves of the scented geraniums. The scented varieties are also edible, and their petals make a delightful addition to a cake or salad. From peach, cinnamon and rose scents, some of our favourites include *P. tomentosum* with its delightfully velvety leaves and peppermint scent, and *P. odoratissimum* with delicate white flowers and an apple perfume. Citrus-scented *Pelargonium* (*P. crispum*, *P. citronellum* and a number of cultivars) act as a great insect repellent to keep the mozzies at bay on your balcony.

Most *Pelargonium* species are native to southern Africa, so while they are often heat and drought tolerant, they are not frost hardy. Definitely happiest outdoors, *Pelargonium* can be brought in for short periods of time for their blooms to be enjoyed. And, given that it grows best in temperate or tropical climates, if things get a little icy during the cooler months you will need to pop it in a sunny but frost-free spot during winter.

Pinch out old stems once flowering is complete to encourage more flower growth, and always be sure to remove dead leaves. Prune every few months during the growing season. Cuttings are super-easy to propagate – simply take a stem cutting and place in water or a pot filled with fresh potting mix. Water regularly while the initial roots are forming, and give it a burst of fertiliser once they have established.

Having soaked up an abundance of light through spring and summer, some plants have only just accumulated enough energy to bloom once autumn arrives. These so-called late bloomers still enjoy plenty of pollinators, and have fewer competitors for them.

autumn

FLOWERS autumn to winter
FAMILY Asphodelaceae
LIGHT filtered/part shade
WATER low to moderate
SOIL coarse + sandy/well draining
POSITION indoor/balcony
FROST HARDY no
EXPERT LEVEL novice

ALOE 'VENUS'

Aloe

Aloe

Hello aloe! These succulents have gloriously dramatic foliage and even more fabulous flowers. And boy, are they prolific, with over 500 known species in the genus.

You may be most familiar with *Aloe vera*, which has been used as a herbal medicine for thousands of years, and whose gooey sap has probably healed your sunburn after a day spent outdoors. But be warned – there are a few toxic species, so be sure of what you've got at hand before rubbing yourself with their juices. *A. ballyi*, *A. elata* and *A. ruspoliana* are the ones to avoid.

Most aloes will bloom for months at a time. Their striking flowers are tubular, densely clustered and hang from the leafless flower stems which stand proud above the architectural leaves. The hybrid pictured here will flower for up to six months and should attract birds, bees and butterflies if planted outdoors. Venus's striking red to white flowers follow one another for a long period over autumn and winter. Other aloe flowers range from bright yellows to oranges and pinks.

Aloe is a low-maintenance member of the plant gang and is more likely to be killed by overwatering and too much fussing than anything else. While most aloes will require you to keep the watering to a minimum and hold off even further in winter, others, such as the dramatic spiral aloe (*A. polyphylla*), can handle a more moderate drink. Most within the genus love bright, filtered light, with lots of gentle morning rays. Cactus potting mix will give you the best results and surrounding the plant with pebbles will make it feel right at home. They will rarely need repotting.

In full flush, this profuse bloomer and all-round excellent house plant is a joyful sight, bringing a serious splash of colour.

The lush cascading foliage of *Nematanthus strigillosus* should be kept out of direct sun and is best displayed in a hanging planter or flowing down from a shelf indoors. It will be equally happy on a covered balcony with dappled shade and plenty of bright light. With a tendency to grow nice and long, it is beneficial to keep the plant well groomed, regularly pinching back stems to encourage bushiness and blooms.

Humidity is appreciated and, during the warmer months in particular, a consistent watering schedule that keeps them relatively moist is ideal. As the plant grows epiphytically in its native environment, it is important to ensure that the potting mix is very well draining. Reducing watering in winter can help to stimulate flowering.

Nematanthus strigillosus

With delightful orange-red flowers that appear like little leaping goldfish, there is no question about the origins of the goldfish plant's common name.

Goldfish plant

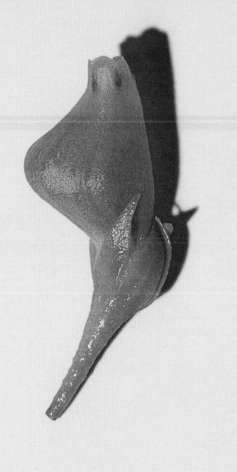

FLOWERS spring to autumn
FAMILY Gesneriaceae
LIGHT filtered/part shade
WATER moderate
SOIL well draining
POSITION indoor/balcony
FROST HARDY no
EXPERT LEVEL novice

autumn

CATTLEYA SP.

Cattleya orchid

Often referred to as the queen of the orchids, this plant's fragrant, showy flowers come in many shapes and colour combinations.

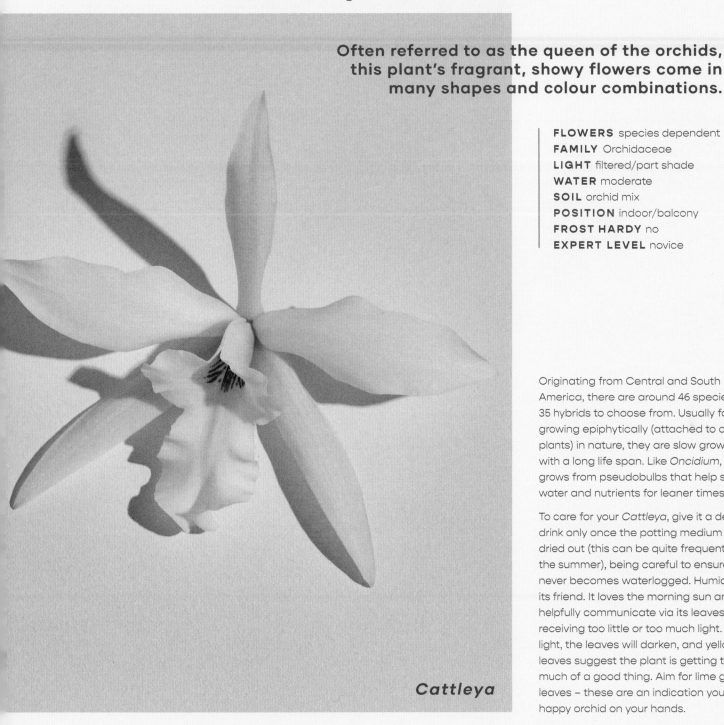

Cattleya

FLOWERS species dependent
FAMILY Orchidaceae
LIGHT filtered/part shade
WATER moderate
SOIL orchid mix
POSITION indoor/balcony
FROST HARDY no
EXPERT LEVEL novice

Originating from Central and South America, there are around 46 species and 35 hybrids to choose from. Usually found growing epiphytically (attached to other plants) in nature, they are slow growers with a long life span. Like *Oncidium*, it grows from pseudobulbs that help store water and nutrients for leaner times.

To care for your *Cattleya*, give it a deep drink only once the potting medium has dried out (this can be quite frequent in the summer), being careful to ensure it never becomes waterlogged. Humidity is its friend. It loves the morning sun and will helpfully communicate via its leaves if it is receiving too little or too much light. In low light, the leaves will darken, and yellowing leaves suggest the plant is getting too much of a good thing. Aim for lime green leaves – these are an indication you have a happy orchid on your hands.

FLOWERS species
dependent, largely autumn
FAMILY Orchidaceae
LIGHT filtered
WATER moderate
SOIL orchid mix
POSITION indoor
FROST HARDY no
EXPERT LEVEL novice

ONCIDIUM 'TWINKLE' IN A TWO SQUIRRELS HANDMADE POT

Dancing lady orchid

Producing long sprays of a plethora of petite flowers, *Oncidium* is affectionately described by many florists as the spray orchid but it is more commonly known as the dancing lady orchid for the way its blooms resemble the swishing skirts of dancing maidens.

Oncidium

Oncidium is mostly seen in shades of yellow and brown, but white, pink, red, green and purple blooms are emerging, along with some scented varieties.

This large and diverse orchid genus is very adaptable and can grow in a variety of different environments, conditions and habitats. This makes it a perfect orchid for beginners.

Oncidium needs an abundance of filtered light, humidity and airflow. As it is mostly epiphytic, it appreciates a very well draining potting medium. While it is relatively drought tolerant, thin-leaved species should be watered more frequently than those with thick, fleshy leaves.

Exposing the plants to cooler night-time temperatures will facilitate flowering. Under the right conditions, it can flower up to three times a year on the same spike, so avoid cutting it off once spent.

There are currently over 1000 *Oncidium* orchid hybrids. *Oncidium* 'Twinkle' is a petite beauty created using *O. cheirophorum* and *O. ornithorhynchum*. This profuse bloomer delights with its ability to produce its delightfully petite flowers year round (but predominantly in autumn).

One of our favourites, *Paphiopedilum*, commonly known as Venus slipper orchid, has flowers that stand to attention high above its fan of leaves in the most charming way. *Paphiopedilum* comes in a huge variety of colours, patterns and versions of its slipper-like shape. The leaves, which are often mottled light and dark green, provide ongoing entertainment when the plant is not in bloom.

Pronounced 'paff-ee-oh-ped-ih-lum' and sometimes referred to by growers as 'paph', its flowers can last anywhere between one and three months. We particularly love the lime green *Paphiopedilum* 'Yi-Ying green coral' and the dramatic stripes and spots of *Paphiopedilum* 'Ruby leopard'.

Paphiopedilum

An incredibly popular and varied group of plants, orchids are a mainstay of many indoor flowering gardens. There are over 25,000 known orchid species that grow natively all over the world.

Venus slipper orchid

FLOWERS autumn to spring
FAMILY Orchidaceae
LIGHT filtered/part shade
WATER moderate
SOIL orchid mix
POSITION indoor/balcony
FROST HARDY no
EXPERT LEVEL
green thumb

These orchids thrive in environments similar to what we enjoy indoors – temperate and consistent. While they can handle a little cold, and are sometimes grown outdoors in gentle climates, they tend to flower more readily indoors.

Unlike many other orchids, paphs do not have a pseudobulb (an above-ground, bulb-like structure that helps plants store water and nutrients), so they do require a little more frequent watering. When it's time for a drink, your plant will prefer lukewarm water. Use a well-draining orchid mix, which their terrestrial roots can cling to, and ease off on watering during winter when they won't be expending as much moisture and energy.

An occasional dose of extra-diluted indoor or orchid-specific liquid fertiliser will give them the boost they need to bloom. When their long-lasting flowers have eventually expired, cut off the flower spike at the base of the plant. Their leaves will begin to fade and eventually die off. Be sure to cut these off at their base once they have turned brown. Your plant should have pushed up a pup or two – this will replace the original plant and will hopefully produce more flowers if its care requirements are consistently met.

autumn

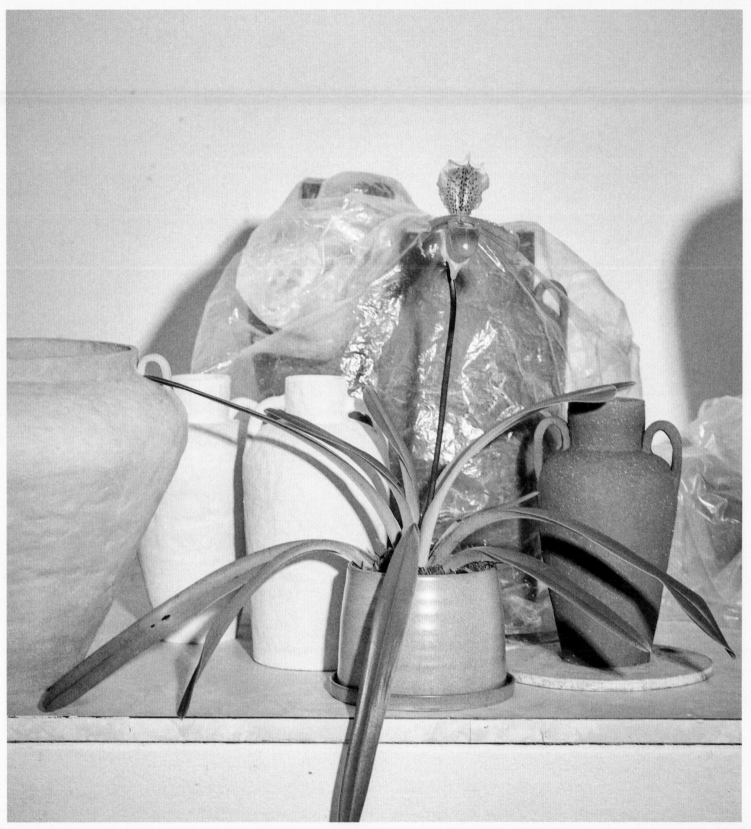

birds + bees / Samantha McIntyre

We first came across Samantha McIntyre on Instagram (@thesodafountain) and were instantly besotted by her wonderfully (and intentionally) wonky, intricately checked ceramics.

As an artist working largely in ceramics and painting, Samantha brings her incredible aesthetic to all aspects of her life, from her art to her home and sprawling rooftop garden. Her connection to bees has encouraged her to grow flowering plants in a way that is harmonious with nature.

WHAT SORT OF PLANTS ARE YOU GROWING ON YOUR ROOFTOP GARDEN?

We have an abundance of succulents and cacti spread out all over the place as well as a few pomegranate shrubs – their little red flowers have just appeared and they are so cute! There is also a lemon tree, a recently found fig tree, along with delphinium that has just flowered, and I'm trying to cultivate a new dahlia plant.

WE LOVE THE NOTION OF GARDENS BEING PASSED FROM TENANT TO TENANT OR OWNER TO OWNER, EACH PLACING THEIR OWN IMPRINT ON THEM. DID YOU INHERIT SOME OF THE GARDEN OR HAS IT ALL BEEN PLANTED BY YOU?

We inherited most of the garden from the owner. When we first moved in, it was overgrown with weeds. We sent her before and after pictures of my weeding escapade and she was thrilled. We've

ABOVE: SAM POSES WITH A PETITE *PHALAENOPSIS*   RIGHT: HER UNIQUE HOME IS FILLED WITH THOUGHTFULLY CHOSEN FURNITURE AND INTERESTING OBJECTS

ABOVE: AN *OXALIS* IN BLOOM   CENTRE: CUT BLOOMS ADORN THE INTERIORS   RIGHT: A RED POMEGRANATE FLOWER IN THE ROOFTOP GARDEN BURSTS INTO LIFE

added a few flowering plants like easter daisies and delphiniums and lavender, and the grasses in the pond, which have seeded. We have been tending to the original garden with lots of love.

CAN YOU OFFER ANY TIPS FOR GROWING IN A SUN-FILLED, INNER-CITY LOCATION?

Plenty of water on those very hot days when there is no sun protection for your plants and always make sure there is a water source for your bees and birds.

WHAT ROLE DO BEES PLAY IN YOUR LIFE? HOW DO THEY IMPACT HOW YOU GARDEN AND RELATE TO NATURE?

Bees are very important to me, not only because they offer a vital role in the ecosystem, but also because they have become a meditative practice for my mental health. Beekeeping is always slow and considered and you have to be very present when opening a hive or you can get stung. The buzzing vibrations of these beauties among the sounds of nature and the city is very calming. I just love it, and the bees, so much. Watching them sit on the plants in the pond – they land to drink from the plants so that they don't drown – is very calming and a great way to remember that life isn't all bad. We bought more flowering plants so the bees would have a local food source on the rooftop and the plants have doubled in size and the flowers come back more frequently. This is why bees are so important. They are my heroes in more than one way.

WHAT CAN WE DO TO HELP KEEP OUR INSECT POPULATIONS HAPPY AND HEALTHY?

Never use pesticides and, if you have a sick plant, research natural methods to treat it. Always leave a safe water source out for your insects to land and drink from and plant flowering gems from both native and introduced species so your native bees and buzzing pollinators have something to feed from and pollinate. If you see a swarm of bees in spring, always call your local beekeeper and NEVER allow them to be exterminated. Swarms are so beautiful – it is the bee super-organism dividing from its mother hive to expand and reproduce. We love collecting swarms and giving them a safe, new home.

"Bees are very important to me, not only because they offer a vital role in the ecosystem, but also because they have become a meditative practice for my mental health."

YOUR HOME IS A BEAUTIFUL, ROMANTIC COLLECTION OF FURNITURE, ART AND OBJECTS. HAS MUCH PLANNING GONE INTO THE INTERIOR STYLING OR IS IT MORE OF AN ONGOING, NATURAL PROCESS?

Some things, like our dining table and the antique cupboards, we inherited from our landlord and the rest I've been collecting over the years. I've rearranged the house once or twice to get everything where it feels the best to me after a few weeks of imagination. I suppose it's mostly intuitive. I love having multiple places to sit or lie, and being able to move into patches of sunshine throughout the day is important to me (and my cats). Art and random objects complete not only a space but those missing places in your soul.

YOU ARE WELL KNOWN FOR YOUR WONDERFULLY ORGANIC SHAPED VESSELS COVERED IN INTRICATE CHECKS. THE LITTLE EGGCUPS ARE A PARTICULAR FAVOURITE OF OURS. (WE ALSO SWOON EVERY TIME WE SEE THE STRAWBERRY VASE!) CAN YOU TELL US A LITTLE ABOUT YOUR PROCESS? DOES NATURE EVER INFORM YOUR WORK?

My desk is plopped in front of a big window that looks out at the garden, our beehives and the city, so I'm always daydreaming and watching this scene while I'm building my vessels. My work is very dependent on my mood – if I'm feeling flat or uninspired, I try to avoid attempting to build because I could spend two hours building a large bowl just to have it collapse, which is very demotivating. On the flip side, when I feel sad, glazing my checks makes me feel safe and light.

WHO ARE SOME OTHER CERAMICISTS AND ARTISTS YOU LOVE?

Cy Twombly, Simone Bodmer-Turner, Cécile Daladier, Harley Weir, Anna Karina, Ruth Asawa, Salvador Dali, Picasso, Andy Warhol, Jean-Michel Basquiat x forever, Guy Bourdin and many more.

ABOVE AND RIGHT: SAM'S HANDMADE CERAMICS, PAINSTAKINGLY PAINTED BY HAND, ARE SCATTERED THROUGHOUT HER HOME

This petite beauty is a classic ornamental plant that has been decorating homes for hundreds of years. It has delicate, generally downward-facing flowers in a variety of white, pink, red and purple hues. Its attractive leaves can be round, angular or heart-shaped, and are often patterned in different shades of green or silver. Some varieties are even delightfully perfumed. In nature you'll find it on alpine mountainsides and across the Mediterranean, and there is even an outlying species in Somalia.

Cyclamen
Sowbread

FLOWERS species dependant
FAMILY Primulaceae
LIGHT filtered/
full shade/part shade
WATER low to moderate
SOIL well draining/
moisture retaining
POSITION indoor/balcony
FROST HARDY yes
EXPERT LEVEL novice

There are two general types of *Cyclamen*: the indoor-loving, so-called florist's cyclamen, most often a hybrid of *C. persicum*, which flowers from autumn to spring, and the hardier, outdoor varieties, such as *C. purpurascens*, *C. hederifolium* or *C. coum,* some of which also flower in summer.

Indoors, your cyclamen will need a cool but still slightly humid spot with lots of filtered light. Although sometimes considered a throwaway plant once flowering is complete, this seems terribly wasteful – why not give it a little care and enjoy it year after year.

As it grows from a tuber, it is important not to overwater your cyclamen, or you'll risk rot. Give your plant a drink once the top 2–5 cm (¾–2 in) of soil has dried out. Water directly onto the potting mix, avoiding the leaves, as this can also contribute to rot. On the flip side, droopy leaves or flowers are a sure sign it's very thirsty. It's best not to let it get to this point.

Deadhead from the base of the stem as each flower or leaf begins to fade. We like the twist-and-push or tug method, making sure you don't leave any remnants.

Cyclamen enters dormant periods after flowering. If yours is a winter-flowering plant, as most indoor varieties are, stop watering as the foliage begins to die back. Place it in a cool dry position, or plant it in the garden (if you're lucky enough to have one). Water sparingly until the weather begins to cool again. You can then return your plant to its regular position, fertilise it, and recommence a regular watering schedule.

Hardier outdoor cyclamen, closer to those found in the wild, will enjoy a spot on a balcony that receives lots of diffuse light. Indoor or outdoor, they like being somewhat rootbound so only repot them every few years, into a marginally larger pot.

The delicate, open-faced blooms of the Japanese anemone form on wiry stems that sit above its attractive foliage. With varieties that are either pure white, light pink or a darker magenta, the petal-like sepals frame a dramatic golden flush of stamens. It is the beautiful way the blooms dance in the wind that inspired one of its common names, Japanese windflower.

Eriocapitella thrives in cooler climates, but will also do well in temperate regions. It enjoys partially shaded conditions, but does require some dappled afternoon or direct morning sun. The appearance of the flowers as the heat of summer begins to wane heralds the changing of the seasons. Once flowering is complete, remove the flower stalks and tidy up any sad-looking foliage by snipping it off at the base of the plant. This will ensure your plant continues to look neat, avoids rotting issues and, most importantly, helps to promote new foliage growth.

Eriocapitella is an avid grower and will reproduce easily via seeds and rhizomes. If you want to keep it in check, remove seed heads before they mature and cut back any new rhizomatous colonies that appear. This isn't a great problem for us, as we're kind of obsessed with this plant!

Eriocapitella

A collection of six similar looking species, the *Eriocapitella* genus (commonly referred to as Japanese anemone or Japanese windflower) includes the popular *Eriocapitella hupehensis* and *E. japonica*. Originating in Asia, this herbaceous perennial has long held a special place in our hearts.

Japanese anemone

FLOWERS late
summer to autumn
FAMILY Ranunculaceae
LIGHT part shade
WATER moderate
SOIL moisture retaining/
well draining
POSITION balcony
FROST HARDY yes
EXPERT LEVEL novice

Adding edible plants to your balcony garden is both beautiful and practical. Who doesn't love the idea of reaching out their window for some herbs to add to a salad or sweet fruit to snack on? Strawberries are a great addition to a container garden as they produce sweet little flowers before fruiting – all without requiring much space.

FLOWERS late autumn to winter
FAMILY Rosaceae
LIGHT full sun
WATER moderate
SOIL well draining/ moisture retaining
POSITION balcony
FROST HARDY yes, but requires protection
EXPERT LEVEL novice

Fragaria
Strawberry

The taste of strawberries brings back vivid memories for Sophia of learning to grow plants in her Nonno's garden, and more recently, foraging for them with the younger members of her family in the Swiss Alps. Kids find so much pleasure in picking and eating them, so they make a great plant to begin teaching them the joys of growing your own food.

There are about 20 species of strawberry, along with many hybrids and cultivars all arising from the rose family. Not technically a berry, rather an aggregate fruit, our pick is the petite and seriously flavourful alpine strawberry (*Fragaria vesca*), which has also been bred in white (*F. vesca* 'White soul') for something more unusual.

A more classic choice is something like *Fragaria* x *ananassa* 'Rubygem', which should produce lots of tasty fruit. All of these have classic white flowers, although some other interesting cultivars have pink and even red blooms.

Most species will start to bloom in late autumn or early winter, once the days shorten to less than 12 hours. The flowers slowly turn into fruit as the weather warms. Strawberries require a lot of sun and good airflow to survive. They do best in temperate environments and many species can handle frost if they are in a semi-protected environment. They have a shallow root system but require a nutrient-dense potting mix, so you'll need to add compost to the pot along with a regular dose of fertiliser. A tomato-specific fertiliser works well. Mulching around the plant will help it retain moisture and ensure any fruit is kept off the soil once they appear.

The delicious berries can be prone to getting eaten by snails and other pests, so set up a small bowl filled with beer to trap any would-be predators, and cover with a cloche if you need to deter birds.

FLOWERS autumn to spring
FAMILY Theaceae
LIGHT part shade
WATER moderate to high
SOIL well draining/camellia mix
POSITION balcony
FROST HARDY yes
EXPERT LEVEL green thumb

CAMELLIA SASANQUA 'PARPETWHI'

Camellia

With evergreen foliage and long-lasting flowers, camellias have been grown successfully in pots for hundreds of years.

The two most common species are *Camellia sasanqua* and *C. japonica*. *C. sasanqua* produces smaller, more delicate flowers but a greater bounty of them, and can tolerate a bit more sun but are not very cold hardy. It generally flowers from autumn to winter, while *C. japonica* flowers last from autumn to spring.

There are a lot of mad camellia lovers out there who have helped to breed an incredible 20,000 plus cultivars. Their flowers range in colour from white through to deep pink, reds and yellows, and mottled mixes of all of the above, and grow in various forms from single petal to blousy peony-like blooms. The abundant 'Parpetwhi' flower (pictured) is lightly perfumed with white petals and a yellow heart. It has been bred as a smaller, compact bush – just right for pots.

Camellias require a specific pH to thrive: acidic, between 5.0 and 6.5. Most nurseries should stock camellia-specific potting mix, and it's worth providing your plant with this correct base to grow in. This well-draining potting mix will dry out relatively quickly, so keep an eye on your plant and give it a deep watering when the top 2 cm (¾ in) of the potting mix has dried. They can also be mulched to help retain moisture, being sure to keep a gap between the mulch and trunk to prevent moisture build-up at the base that can lead to collar rot. In the dormant season, they need a half-strength water-soluble fertiliser formulated for acid-loving plants.

Camellias can tolerate partial sun to full shade but need protection from the hot sun. Straight after flowering, give your plant a gentle prune. Don't wait too long or you run the risk of chopping off healthy new growth or flower buds. Cutting at least 2.5 cm (1 in) off the end of each branch will result in a much bushier plant when it starts to grow again. Repot every two to three years.

Some of our favourite cultivars include the simple, single white petal of *C. japonica* 'Alba simplex', the deep red of *C. japonica* 'Black magic' and the red stripes of the *C. japonica* 'Tinker toy'.

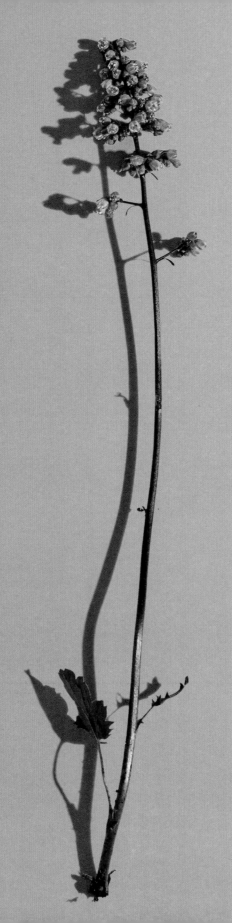

HEUCHERA 'BLONDIE'

Coral bells

Vigorous and easy to grow, this attractive, ruffled, colourfully leaved plant also produces tall flower spikes that stand proudly above the crown.

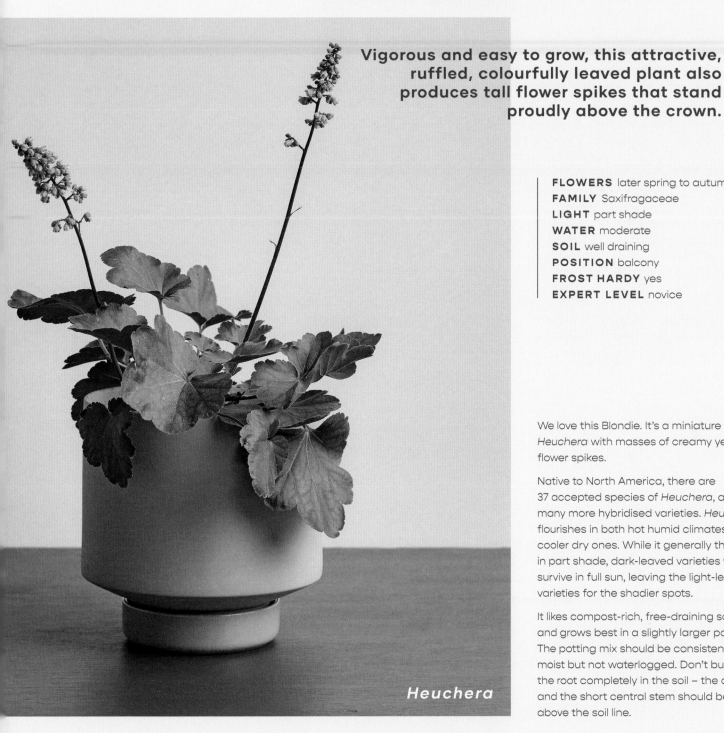

Heuchera

FLOWERS later spring to autumn
FAMILY Saxifragaceae
LIGHT part shade
WATER moderate
SOIL well draining
POSITION balcony
FROST HARDY yes
EXPERT LEVEL novice

We love this Blondie. It's a miniature *Heuchera* with masses of creamy yellow flower spikes.

Native to North America, there are 37 accepted species of *Heuchera*, and many more hybridised varieties. *Heuchera* flourishes in both hot humid climates and cooler dry ones. While it generally thrives in part shade, dark-leaved varieties will survive in full sun, leaving the light-leaved varieties for the shadier spots.

It likes compost-rich, free-draining soil and grows best in a slightly larger pot. The potting mix should be consistently moist but not waterlogged. Don't bury the root completely in the soil – the crown and the short central stem should be above the soil line.

Dropping temperatures and shorter days can create the perfect conditions for cold-hardy plants to come to life. While some will experience a period of dormancy in winter, others are just gearing up to put on a display to brighten the greyest of days.

winter

CYMBIDIUM SP.

Cymbidium

Boat orchid

Elegant and long-lasting, *Cymbidium* is an excellent cool-season bloomer that grows widely in the mountainous areas of India, South-East Asia and Australia.

FLOWERS winter
FAMILY Orchidaceae
LIGHT filtered/part shade
WATER moderate
SOIL well draining/orchid mix
POSITION indoor/balcony
FROST HARDY no
EXPERT LEVEL novice

Cymbidium has been selectively bred and hybridised over the last 100 or so years, and its blooms can now be found in an array of colours, sizes and shapes, from deep chocolates through to the brightest of yellows and from 1 cm (¾ in) to over 15 cm (6 in) across. Flowering in winter, triggered by lower temperatures and a reduction in water, cyms, as they're fondly referred to, are delightfully hardy, easy to care for and gorgeous to boot.

Growing beautifully in containers both indoors and on sheltered balconies, *Cymbidium* will do best in a position with lots of bright, indirect light. Direct harsh sun will burn its leaves while a lack of light will see the leaves turn dark green. Finding the right balance is key. Ensure the plant is potted in a well-draining orchid-specific mix and keep it relatively moist, particularly during its active growth period, reducing watering slightly in autumn and winter. For the best blooms, apply a regular dose of liquid fertiliser throughout spring and summer. Adding a touch of dolomite lime (a limestone compound that contains beneficial calcium and magnesium) to the potting medium in spring will provide alkalinity to the soil that will give cyms some extra pep!

Cymbidium orchids can live a long happy life with the right care, producing more and more flower spikes year after year. Their beautiful blooms are also long-lasting, appearing from four to 12 weeks, giving you plenty of time to savour their exotic display.

This sweet and undemanding plant will bloom most of the year, but the small daisy-like flowers are most abundant in winter. Appearing as single flowers, like other daisies they are in fact a cluster of tiny flowers that grow about 2.5 cm (1 in) above their small pickle-shaped leaves.

Light is key for encouraging blooms as well as the overall health of *Othonna capensis*. A bright spot indoors with access to some morning sun but sheltered from harsh afternoon rays is good, and the same applies to an outdoor position. The amount of light will determine the colour of the leaves. With stronger sun exposure (and a lack of fertiliser) the green foliage will take on a darker, redder appearance.

Othonna capensis is a beautifully easy plant to grow and, once established, is fairly drought tolerant. Avoid soggy roots that can lead to rot by watering deeply and then allowing the soil to dry out. Containers and hanging pots are perfect for this trailer, which can spread in abundance if allowed to. Just be sure to opt for a well-draining potting mix and pots with adequate drainage.

Othonna capensis

With a common name like 'little pickles', you would expect nothing less than a cute-as-a-button plant and *Othonna capensis* does not disappoint. This delicate succulent that grows natively in South Africa sports vibrant purple stems and rich green foliage that contrast its dainty bright yellow flowers perfectly.

Little pickles

FLOWERS year round,
peaking in winter
FAMILY Asteraceae
LIGHT filtered/part shade
WATER low
SOIL well draining
POSITION indoor/balcony
FROST HARDY no
EXPERT LEVEL novice

RHIPSALIS PILOCARPA

Rhipsalis pilocarpa

Hairy stemmed rhipsalis

The covering of tiny white hairs on its thin pendulous stems has given this popular house plant its common name. *Rhipsalis pilocarpa* is an epiphytic jungle cactus, originating from the tropical rainforests around Brazil where it grows high up in the tree branches. Thankfully for us it also lives very happily indoors or on a covered balcony.

FLOWERS winter
FAMILY Cactaceae
LIGHT filtered/part shade
WATER moderate
SOIL well draining/
orchid or epiphyte-specific mix
POSITION indoor/balcony
FROST HARDY no
EXPERT LEVEL novice

An award winner, with a Royal Horticultural Society's garden of merit to its name, *Rhipsalis pilocarpa* is low maintenance and beautiful to boot. With consistent watering and fertilising during the growing season, heavily reduced once temperatures start to drop, it will bloom profusely, producing delightfully fragranced white flowers at the end of its branches. Plenty of bright but indirect light will also facilitate flowering.

Unlike desert-dwelling cactus, a potting mix that retains some moisture is best. Opt for a medium that is specific for orchids, bromeliads and other epiphytic plants. Also in contrast to its sun-loving brethren, a position sheltered from direct rays is best to avoid burning the stems.

While the stems can be delicate and easily knocked off, they are equally easy to propagate and turn into new plants to gift or add to your own collection. Simply pop them back into the soil and they should root in due course.

This striking epiphytic jungle cactus hails from the coastal mountains of south-eastern Brazil and thrives in shady conditions with plenty of humidity. Very distinct in appearance to its desert-dwelling relatives, the stems of the plant resemble short leaf-like sections with pointed teeth, joined at short intervals to each other. The striking blooms, which form at the joints and ends of the stems, come in a myriad of colours from white, pink and yellow through to red and purple, depending on the cultivar.

Providing cooler temperatures and long periods of darkness overnight, along with lots of bright, indirect light throughout the day will help your plant flower.

When in bloom, you can increase watering slightly but always allow at least 2–5 cm (¾–2 in) of potting mix to dry out between drinks. A well-draining mix will ensure roots are aerated and help stave off any possible rot that can occur from overwatering.

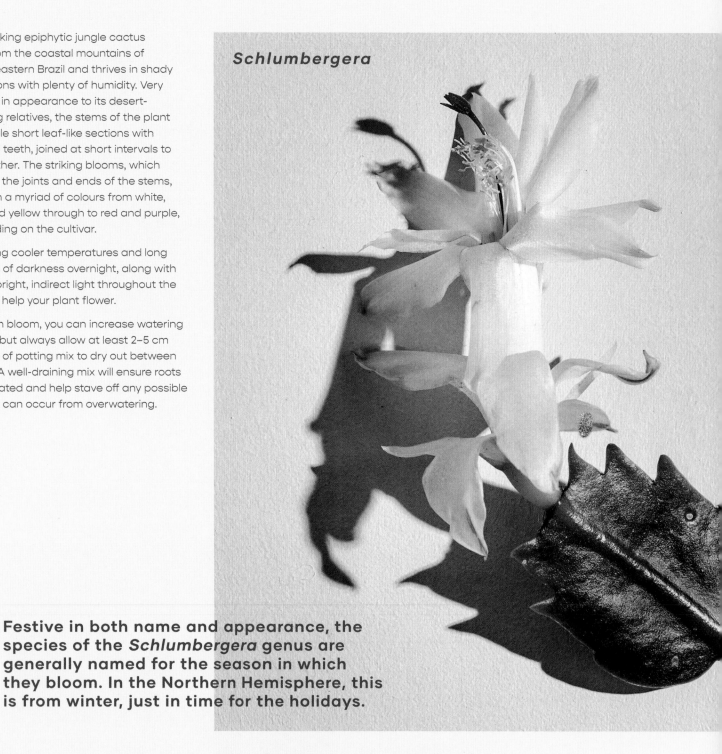

Schlumbergera

Festive in both name and appearance, the species of the *Schlumbergera* genus are generally named for the season in which they bloom. In the Northern Hemisphere, this is from winter, just in time for the holidays.

Holiday cactus

FLOWERS winter
FAMILY Cactaceae
LIGHT filtered/part shade
WATER moderate
SOIL well draining
POSITION indoor/balcony
FROST HARDY no
EXPERT LEVEL novice

KALANCHOE BLOSSFELDIANA IN A CURVACEOUS ADELE MACER POT

Kalanchoe blossfeldiana

Florist kalanchoe

Known by several common names – florist kalanchoe, Christmas kalanchoe and Madagascar widow's thrill, to name a few – this bright and bubbly succulent with vividly coloured blooms makes a cheery addition to any indoor or balcony garden. And even better, this easy-care plant can bloom freely for two to six months, so there's plenty of time to enjoy the show.

FLOWERS late autumn to winter
FAMILY Crassulaceae
LIGHT filtered/direct/
part shade/full sun
WATER low to moderate
SOIL coarse + sandy
POSITION indoor/balcony
FROST HARDY no
EXPERT LEVEL novice

Native to Madagascar and tropical Africa, which explains one of those common monikers, *Kalanchoe blossfeldiana* enjoys plenty of bright light and a coarse potting mix specific to cacti and succulents. Storing water in its chubby leaves, it is relatively drought tolerant and enjoys drying out between watering. Feeding it with a half-strength liquid fertiliser monthly in spring and summer will promote beautiful blooms for years to come.

Just like cyclamens and poinsettias, short days and cooler temperatures can trigger *Kalanchoe blossfeldiana* to flower, which means it is often in bloom over the holiday period in the Northern Hemisphere. Given the Christmas blooms and ready availability, it is a popular gift. Sadly, this can also mean it is not given the (minimal) attention it needs to thrive and the plants are often discarded once through their flowering period. By removing spent blooms and simulating short days by managing the hours of natural light the plant receives in a day, the flowers may return in abundance for a much longer time.

BRYOPHYLLUM DELAGOENSE

Bryophyllum delagoense

Mother of millions

An intriguing and unusual succulent, *Bryophyllum delagoense* (syn. *Kalanchoe delagoensis*) is commonly known as mother of millions or the chandelier plant or both pertaining to its striking growth habit.

FLOWERS late autumn to winter
FAMILY Crassulaceae
LIGHT full sun
WATER low
SOIL well draining
POSITION balcony
FROST HARDY no
EXPERT LEVEL novice

Hundreds of tiny leaf-like structures line the outer edges of its incredible leaves. These plantlets detach from the mother plant, allowing it to rapidly reproduce. A container makes the perfect home for this prolific grower, which can quickly overtake a garden if allowed the freedom to do so.

The somewhat elusive bell-shaped flowers appear red, orange or pink and grow pendulously in tight clusters at the top of long stems. While this striking succulent requires little attention to thrive, it will appreciate some special care to encourage its beautiful, bright flowers to burst forth. A daily period of sustained darkness, around 14 hours, followed by ten hours of very bright light, along with limited water, are some of the specific requirements that need to be met.

It's worth noting that all parts of this plant are poisonous if ingested, but especially the flowers. This is why *B. delagoense* is not a common house plant and should be kept away from animals and curious children. In some areas, this species is considered a noxious weed and there are restrictions placed on the growing and selling of it. Be sure to check on its status in your area.

FLOWERS winter to spring
FAMILY Gesneriaceae
LIGHT filtered
WATER moderate
SOIL African violet mix
POSITION indoor
FROST HARDY no
EXPERT LEVEL novice

STREPTOCARPUS IONANTHUS SUBSP. VELUTINUS

African violet

This petite plant is a classic of the flowering indoor plant game. Originally from eastern Africa, it is the perfect fit for small spaces that need a little hit of life, and is considered a traditional gift to mothers in some cultures.

Streptocarpus

The fuzzy ovate leaves of *Streptocarpus* grow from a central cluster, providing a cosy backdrop for the bright flowers. Most often purple, which is where the plant gets its common name, the flowers can also be found in pinks, reds, whites, yellows and even a rare black.

Although it will tolerate lower light conditions, it will not bloom unless given plenty of filtered light. Be sure to keep it near a window, but not too close to any cold glass or draughts. Rotating the plant regularly will help to ensure even growth.

When watering, avoid getting the leaves wet, instead angling the watering can directly into the potting mix. Lukewarm water is best, and it will also benefit from warm temperatures indoors and a bit of added humidity.

Pinch off dead flowers and yellow leaves and brush the happy leaves regularly to stop dust building up. Fertilise fortnightly during the active flowering periods with a specific liquid fertiliser, always erring on the side of caution by over-diluting.

FLOWERS winter to spring
FAMILY Ranunculaceae
LIGHT part shade
WATER moderate
SOIL well draining
POSITION balcony
FROST HARDY yes
EXPERT LEVEL novice

HELLEBORUS 'ANNA'S RED'

Hellebore

Helleborus **is a much-loved perennial, flowering when and where many other plants do not – through the frost and in shaded spots. Because of this, it is sometimes called the winter rose, although it is far from related to the rose family.**

It may seem subtle from afar, but up close, the long-lasting flowers of *Helleborus* bloom in a dazzling array of colours from whites, yellows, greens and plums to pinks and almost black. Hybridisation has created frilly, double-flowering plants and many unusually mottled and splattered petals.

Most hellebores produce shy, downward-facing blooms, so their pots are best placed in an elevated position to best admire them. In nature they are often found growing at the base of deciduous trees, so attempt to mimic their natural environment by giving them gentle sunlight during the colder seasons to encourage flowering, and moving them to a fully shaded spot when things warms up. If the conditions aren't right, hellebores often find themselves prone to aphids, so be sure not to leave them out in the sun in summer as this will weaken the plant and its immune system. If you do find your plant has fallen victim to these pests, treat it with a natural pesticide. Summer is also a good time to add mulch to the pot, (making sure to keep it clear of the base of the plant) to keep the potting mix cool and moist. When winter arrives, add compost to the potting mix to encourage a strong flowering.

When potting, choose a deep pot to allow the strong roots space to grow. Use a pot that will allow easy repotting when the time comes, as the roots don't enjoy being disturbed. During the growing season, give the plant a liquid feed every two weeks, and once flowering is complete, remove any dead stems at the base of the plant and give it a gentle prune to encourage fresh growth. *Helleborus* is quite toxic, so be sure to keep it clear of curious pets and kids.

Some of our favourites include the pure white *H. niger*, the black as night *Helleborus × hybridus* 'Double black', the more erect flowering *Helleborus* 'Ivory prince' and the deep plum *Helleborus* 'Anna's red'.

Viola × wittrockiana often comes with contrasting dark splotches, reminiscent of panda bears, or thin lines that fan out from the centre like eyelashes. At times this plant is the only thing adding colour to our winter garden, and for this we especially appreciate it.

Garden pansies look great mass planted in a container or, if you don't have as much space, a single little plant allowed to shine in a small pot makes the sweetest addition to your garden. They will generally grow to be about 20 cm (8 in) high. If you're after taller flower stems for cutting and arranging, potting them among other plants will ensure they grow tall in their effort to jostle for attention and light. We have ours co-planted with mint and strawberries.

If you're able to show restraint, the plant will benefit from having its first buds pinched back to allow it to direct more energy into establishing itself, ensuring a stronger flourish of flowers later. Continue to deadhead the flowers once they do appear to encourage a longer blooming period. They will probably die back as the weather warms.

All parts of the plant are edible, and the flowers make a pretty decoration placed fresh on cakes or baked into shortbread cookies.

Viola × wittrockiana

A hybrid plant cultivated especially as a garden flower, the garden pansy is a vibrant and sweet-natured bloomer. *Viola × wittrockiana* is the origin for all garden pansies, of which there are thousands in a myriad of colour combinations.

Garden pansy

FLOWERS winter to spring
FAMILY Violaceae
LIGHT full sun
WATER high
SOIL well draining
POSITION balcony
FROST HARDY yes
EXPERT LEVEL novice

index

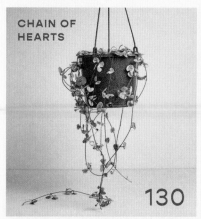

CHAIN OF HEARTS 130

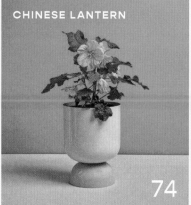

CHINESE LANTERN 74

COLUMBINE 85

CONEFLOWER 145

CORAL BELLS 189

50

CORNFLOWER

COSMOS 53

CRANESBILL 67

DAHLIA 138

DANCING LADY ORCHID 167

EMERALD
FOREST
69

FALSE SHAMROCK
79

FLAMINGO FLOWER
44

FLORIST KALANCHOE
201

GARDEN PANSY
208

GERANIUM
156

GIANT CHANDELIER PLANT
77

137

GOLDFISH PLANT
162

HAIRY STEMMED
RHIPSALIS
197

GOLDEN MARGUERITE

HELLEBORE  207

HEN AND CHICKS  64

HOLIDAY CACTUS  198

HORTENSIA  146

JAPANESE ANEMONE  182

KANGAROO PAW  70

LARKSPUR  86

LAVENDER  113

LITTLE PICKLES  194

MARIGOLD  107

MEALY SAGE  118

MOSS ROSE  134

MOTH ORCHID  90

MOTHER OF MILLIONS
203

MOUSE FLOWER
121

NATIVE VIOLET
82

NODDING VIOLET
149

PEACE LILY
49

PELICAN FLOWER
133

PINK QUILL PLANT
63

127
PLANTAIN LILY

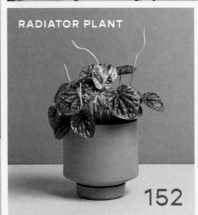
RADIATOR PLANT
152

ROCKTRUMPET
129

ROSE

151

ROSEMARY

117

104

SNOW POPPY

142

SOWBREAD

180

SEASIDE DAISY

STRAWBERRY

184

TULIP

VENUS SLIPPER ORCHID

168

WAX PLANT

124

72

WHITE BATFLOWER

115

index

about the authors

Lauren Camilleri and Sophia Kaplan are the co-founders of Sydney-based online indoor plant and botanical ware store Leaf Supply, the go-to for all things indoor plants.

In the process of building their business, they have become authorities in the indoor plant world. Since 2018, they have published three highly successful (and award-winning) indoor plant books – *Leaf Supply*, *Indoor Jungle* and *Plantopedia* – with Smith Street Books. Available worldwide, the books showcase the pair's passion for sharing their plant knowledge.

Lauren has a background in interior architecture and, along with running Leaf Supply, works as a creative director. Sophia started life in communications and production before changing tack and becoming a floral designer.

They are both totally enamoured by plants and want everyone else to fall in love with them in the same way they have. Through their work they endeavour to empower people with knowledge, helping them gain confidence when it comes to caring for, styling and living with plants. Ultimately their wish is to inspire fellow gardeners, and would-be green thumbs to appreciate and hold value in the incredible wonder and fragility of our natural world.

ABOVE: SOPHIA AND LAUREN IN THE STUDIO OF ARTIST CAROL CRAWFORD   RIGHT: AN *ONCIDIUM* ORCHID AMONG SOME TARA BURKE CERAMICS

Smith Street Books

Published in 2022 by Smith Street Books
Naarm | Melbourne | Australia
smithstreetbooks.com

ISBN: 978-1-92241-785-5

Publisher: Paul McNally
Creative director: Lauren Camilleri
Production: Sophia Kaplan
Photography: Becca Crawford
Horticultural consultant: Jane Rose Lloyd
Additional photography: Sophia Kaplan (p. 132), Jane Rose Lloyd (p. 122) and Jacqui Turk (p. 78)
Editor: Lorna Hendry
Project editor: Aisling Coughlan
Indexer: Helena Holgrem
Proofreader: Pamela Dunne
Printed & bound in China by C&C Offset Printing Co., Ltd.

Book 229

10 9 8 7 6 5 4 3 2 1

FSC
www.fsc.org

MIX
Paper from
responsible sources
FSC® C008047

thank you

We count ourselves very lucky that we get to make these books, but it is only possible with the help of many people. To our publisher, Paul McNally at Smith Street Books, thank you for continuing to give us these opportunities, trusting in us and helping to get our books out to an audience far and wide. To Lorna Hendry, our editor, for patiently and expertly putting together the puzzle pieces of our manuscript and showing such care and attention to detail, we send our warm thanks. Aisling Coughlan, project editor, has helped keep this ship afloat – her guidance has been essential and she is much appreciated.

Becca Crawford, who photographed this book, we are so lucky to have been able to work with you. Shoot days were always such fun and seeing the images you created pop up on the monitor was a constant treat. Thank you. Jane Rose Lloyd, our invaluable horticultural consultant – sorry for the late-night texts and thank you from the bottom of our hearts for loving plants the way you do and sharing all that involves with us.

To the plant people who so generously let us into their homes and minds, thank you for being part of this book. Jane Rose Lloyd (once again) with your enviable greenhouse and sexy nails, Petrina Burrill with your rambling garden and joyful spirit, and Samantha McIntyre whose indelible style and enthusiasm for this project is so appreciated.

We would like to send warm thanks to Tara Burke and Saskia Wilson for allowing us to shoot in their beautiful studio, the one with the magic light. You can see our plants hiding among Tara's ceramics on pages 171 and 221. Special thanks also to Becca's mama, Carol Crawford, who kindly hosted us in her equally fabulous studio, featured in our plant care chapter. Placing our plants among her curvaceous alabaster sculptures was equal parts nerve-wracking and thrilling.

To Alana Scherr, Claire Madiot and Cooper Solberg for holding down the fort in the Leaf Supply studio, allowing us the space to write and shoot this book, thank you lovely ones!

Sophia: Lauren and I have found a lovely rhythm to book-making together. It is a joy working with her and I thank her for it. That she is also an incredible creative director handling the book design is a huge bonus. To my parents, Janice and Lewis, thank you for being eternally supportive, both emotionally and from a practical point of view, helping me to find my way, and allowing me quiet moments to write and produce this book. I love you both dearly. Rosie, my much-loved aunt, thank you for your general enthusiasm and all your plant research. To my partner, Mike, and babies, Rafi and Otis, you are the biggest and best distraction, I love you.

Lauren: With four of these bad boys now under our belt, we've definitely refined our process and it continues to be a joyous if at times all-consuming endeavour. Soph is a fantastic partner in crime and there's no one I'd rather do this work with. A huge thank you to my parents, Richard and Maree, who are my greatest cheerleaders, my husband, Anthony, for his endless patience and support and my crazy, clever, charismatic Frankie, my future fellow plant lady. None of this would be possible without these legends around us.

contributors

We are very grateful to collaborate with such a talented bunch of women, who have made the process of producing this book all the more enjoyable.

JANE ROSE LLOYD, HORTICULTURAL CONSULTANT

Since she opened her plant-filled home to us back in 2019 to appear on the pages of *Indoor Jungle*, Jane Rose Lloyd has become a dear friend and collaborator. In the role of horticultural consultant for *Plantopedia*, her meticulous attention to detail and extensive plant knowledge ensured all the information was spot on and scientifically up to date. With a diploma in horticultural science, she specialises in binomial nomenclature, plant identification and plant selection for niche environments. Her input and general encouragement have always been invaluable, and having her by our side for *Bloom*, once again acting as horticultural consultant, was a joy. Some of her plants feature in our plant profiles and you can read more about Jane and her love of strange plants on pages 94–103.

BECCA CRAWFORD, PHOTOGRAPHER

We have long admired Becca's work from afar, and her return to Australia after years living and working in Berlin was most fortuitous. Her incredible eye and her naturalistic, vibrant, modern style of photography is a perfect match for *Bloom*. Totally embracing our brief and the subject matter, her images vividly encapsulate the magic of the plants and people featured in this book. We're eternally grateful for the opportunity to shoot with her, not only was it fun and inspiring but we now happily count Becca as a friend. Currently based in Melbourne and shooting between Melbourne, Sydney and Berlin, Becca works on editorial, commercial and documentary projects as well as capturing intimate portraits of motherhood.

ROSIE KAPLAN, RESEARCHER

Rosie – researcher extraordinaire (amongst her many other talents) – has always stepped up enthusiastically to help, providing invaluable notes for our plant profiles, along with endless love and encouragement. She first assisted on *Plantopedia* when the sheer size of our manuscript was beginning to overwhelm us, and happily for us came back on board for *Bloom*, helping to shape many of the plant profiles on these pages.